Survivor Benefits

Nasim Nehawandian

DEDICATION

Survivor Benefits is a loving tribute to my beloved husband and the life we created.

Survivor Benefits is dedicated to my fellow human beings who take the care to think, see, and be better versions of themselves en route to our collective evolution.

CONTENTS

ACKNOWLEDGMENTS

I recognize that there are many facets to one's character. I recognize that all of life is a gift to help us blossom. I would like to acknowledge, with love, those selfish individuals who display hurtful judgment in their interactions with others.

I am most grateful to my family and friends who have shown me love and care in my time of need.

I am grateful to Childhood Friend and her mother who encouraged my writing as a venue for my healing.

I am grateful to Kristina Swanson and the Hospice of the Valley for giving me the guidance and hope to carry on.

I am grateful to Kara Grief for providing a group setting where I heal with fellow widowers.

I am grateful to Mana Nahavandian for the creation of *Survivor Benefits* book cover.

Chapter One
Dreadful Mourning

My heart was on the ground.
My mind was in the sky.

With the void of disbelief, I knew that he had not moved since
I had woken up in the middle of the night to lovingly check on
him. Though my heart knew it was real, my mind said it is not.

This cannot be real.
Was he gone?
Had I lost him?

I screamed and cried in my heart for help at the mercy of the
machines and medicines now in our bed and all the way to the
hospital that dreadful unforgettable morning.

Nothing.
No one.
Never again.

For over 24 years We were One.

We lived.
        We loved.
We danced.
        We built.
We fought.
        We compromised.
We understood.
        We protected.
We gave.
        We sacrificed.
We laughed.
        We cried.
We shared.
        We cared.

From this day forth I was no longer We with Him.
Death had done us apart.

—

We did Love.

My last words to him were "good night, I love you." His last words on earth "I love you too" were spoken to our younger daughter whom he had hugged good night after she had expressed her love.

Three kids faced the unbearable that morning. In a synchronized manner, they ran into our master bedroom. Their father laid in bed, void of life. Our son, the oldest, a senior in high school, resuscitating his father until the paramedics arrived. Our daughters terrified cries while holding their father's hand as I try to follow the directions from the 911 operator.

It seemed like a lifetime for the paramedics to finally arrive. Our home is not easy to find. At some point the girls let go of their father's hand to run, find, and guide the paramedics to our home and into our master bedroom. The paramedics had us go to my younger daughter's room. The police arrived. All four of us were in shock and tears. I walked in circles talking to myself.

This can't be.
This can Not be.

It somehow occurred to me to call my older sister. I could not speak. I did not have words. I cried for help. She came to my door. It had also occurred to me to ask my son to call my husband's sister.

The paramedics and police gently and humanely told us that there was nothing more that could be done. My heart knew there was nothing more. My mind could not accept. There has to be something more. Maybe the hospital has better equipment. Maybe the hospital doctors can bring him back. There has to be something more that can be done. I begged and cried for help. The ambulance arrived. So did my nephew who must have locked up the house for us as my older sister drove my kids and me to the hospital.

—

My husband's sister was at the hospital door when we arrived. She saw our faces and realized it was serious. Being at the hospital was a blur. People were coming and going. We ended up in the room where my husband was being held with the hospital pastor. I recall the four of us standing around him as he laid on that bed with his smile.

It was just a bad dream.
Will I wake up?
When will I wake up?

I had to turn towards positivity. I said a memory We had shared and then our kids went around in a circle sharing their memories. I started rambling on about what I would miss the most and our kids took turns sharing what they would miss the most. Each kid had alone time with dad to say goodbye.

It was the five of us together for the last time.
In the background I could feel my older sister, my husband's sister, and my mom in that room.
It was just the five of us for the last time.

Chapter Two
After Shock

My day was a daze.

After the hospital, my kids and I had been taken to my older sister's home. Ultimate Love surrounded us. The five of us had lived with my older sister for a period of almost two years while we were rebuilding our home. So my kids felt right at home. Just one mile away, friends and family had gathered to fill my parents' home with true love.

My friends, even ones I hadn't seen for a long while, somehow appeared. They were there for support. I hadn't realized how much I needed them. I felt blessed to have them around me as they kept bringing me calming teas and caressing me like a baby.

I kept repeating:
He wasn't even 50.
He didn't even make it to 50.
He will not be there when our kids graduate.
He will not be there when our kids get married and have children.
He will not be there to grow old with Me.
He will not be there, ever.

I began to question what could I have done to prevent this from happening? Friends reinforced that it would have been prevented if it could have been prevented. What has happened has happened. This was destiny.

In the late afternoon of our dreadful horrid morning, my husband's general doctor called. I couldn't really comprehend what she was saying. I could comprehend that she was matter of fact. I could comprehend she was innately callous, forcefully attempting to be compassionate. Something about the coroner does not recommend an autopsy. Therefore the insurance company will not cover an autopsy. However, if I would pay out of pocket for an autopsy, the doctors could learn from what had happened.

I did not care about doctors' learning. What had happened had happened. An autopsy will not bring my husband back. I asked if and how an autopsy will help my kids. The reply was that if my husband died of heart disease then my kids would need to eat healthy and be active to prevent heart disease. In my confusion, I handed the phone to my husband's sister.

What is this doctor saying?

Though my mind was not optimally functioning, it did occur to me that my kids were already eating healthy and being active. Months later I found out from our pediatric cardiologist that while an autopsy would not provide much if any information for my kids, genetic testing to find potential mutations would have been very helpful. It hadn't occurred to the Callous Doctor to give me that piece of information.

I couldn't fall asleep all night. My older sister's cat, Tiger, knew something was wrong. Tiger's eyes showed me unconditional love and deep understanding in my confusion of despair.

That first morning I was up and decided to go for a walk. As I stood in front of my older sister's home, I thought of two friends. Ann lived about a mile to the right and Bella lived a half mile to the left of my older sister's home.

I was halfway to Bella's home when I realized that the bottom of my feet had collected little rocks from the asphalt.

Was I barefoot? Yes.
Was I wearing a borrowed nightgown? Yes.

I continued on, only to find Bella must have been out of town since no one was home at such an early hour. Or could it just be that they were asleep and didn't hear my desperate knocks?

I thought, now I will go to Ann. Did I make a mistake? Why didn't I choose to go to Ann's first? It was chilly. Had I forgotten to wear a jacket? As I was walking, my feet started to complain and I found myself at my older sister's home once again.

My older sister couldn't sleep all night either. She had heard me leave. She wanted to give me space yet had been concerned. My older sister suggested that we visit my husband's sister to see how she was holding up.

At my husband's sister's home, it was good to see that her boyfriend had made it up from Los Angeles. They had been together on-and-off for over 16 years. Though she did not believe in marriage, she had decided to have a court wedding for the sake of elders in the family. When she discovered that my husband, our kids, and I would be going on a heritage trip to Iran that winter, she planned her court wedding in Iran during the time we would be there. The five of us had been set to fly to Iran that very morning, that dreadful unbearable morning when life took a different turn. Instead with the devastating news, my husband's parents and his brother's family of four who were in Iran awaiting a wedding, were now on their way back to the United States.

We were all in shock and disbelief. My older sister and my husband's sister's boyfriend were talking in the kitchen and out of sight. Out of nowhere, my husband's sister started talking about money with me. My brain could not wrap around what she was getting at. She said my husband had taken money from "her" family, and this had deeply hurt all of "her" family.

Isn't my husband "her" family?
What was she saying?

If my mind had been clear I would have gotten up to leave her home never to go back. However, I was in a mind fog.

—

11

I proclaimed that my husband was one of the most honest human beings. What are you saying about your own brother?

I went into justification mode. I know our money was tied up in investments and we had to borrow money from my husband's father so we could finish our construction project that had gone over budget. I also know we refinanced and paid back every single penny after construction was over.

I knew my husband would never take a single penny from anyone. That is who he was. In the first year I had known him my husband found $20 cash on the floor of a grocery store that he turned over to their lost and found.

In the 24 years of my being with him, my husband's trustworthiness never waivered.

My husband was also a financial doctor. My parents' entire wealth-being was in his trusted hands which he transformed from brink of bankruptcy to financial prosperity with every single penny accounted for.

Why was she talking about money one day after her brother has passed? Why was she attacking her deceased brother/my husband?

My husband's sister insisted that there were hundreds of thousands of dollars not accounted for. I tried to explain that we had been gifted $100,000 for our new home. She insisted it was money taken and not a gift.

I started shaking.

My older sister realized I was distraught and she came to see what was going on. My husband's sister told my older sister that we were all affected by what has happened. I agreed. Yes you are all affected. However, your lives will continue on as is. It is my life that is upside down. My kids who are fatherless. My future that is uncertain. My older sister took me away and we left.

I was still shaking.

It came to me that I don't know much details about our finances. I never had to worry about money. That was my husband's department. My department was our kids. My job was to make sure we had healthy food and healthy kids. My job was for our kids to be empowered, self-reliant, and loved.

How will I know what to do?
How will I know what we have?
How will I manage?
How will I manage life without him?

I could not stop shaking.
I could not stop looking into nothingness.
I could not stop whispering to myself.
I could not stop.

As my friends rallied around me, it became clear that no one was to leave me alone. I was to be guarded every minute of every day.

Ann sent a care package to my older sister's home that evening. Ann hadn't even known that I should have visited her that morning. The care package had a pouch of lavender and homemade goodies such as lavender tea with dried persimmons. That pouch of lavender became my savior. All I wanted to do was to smell my new lavender pouch.

A couple of days had passed and I was still shaking, staring into nothingness, and whispering to myself. I had my pouch of lavender that I smelled. I had rosary beads that I religiously moved with my thumb.

My husband's birth family came from Iran. I was told that my sisters and parents went to visit my husband's parents upon their arrival. I was at my parents' home when my husband's birth family came for a visit. There was commotion outside. They finally came in. My husband's mother did not respond to my effort of a welcome from my state of disbelief and voidness. My husband's brother responded to me and I hugged him repeating that I loved him.

I joined everyone seated in my parents' living room. I sat there shaking. My husband's mother was glaring at me. My husband's father was disheartened that we had not made our heritage trip to Iran. His words floated in the air. *Bring the kids to Iran. We will take them skiing together.* I was rocking, staring, and counting my rosary beads. My kids were in the room. There were moments of silence.

My husband's father, not a big talker, recounted that his friends had suggested my kids and I move to Iran so he can take care of us. He had told his friends that moving us would be difficult adding that he can take care of us in the United States as well. Words were still floating in the air with no beginning or end.

Pillar Friend, to break the tension, inquired about their trip and how they were holding up. My husband's mother blurted out with hostility that she had tolerated me all these years and with her son gone, she no longer has to. Then my husband's father jumped right into the business of a proper Muslim burial and positioning.

I got up and left into a back room. I had meant no disrespect. I just couldn't bear their conversations.

My husband's sister followed me to see if I was okay. I explained that I was fine. Her parents had every right to be comfortable and talk about what is important to them. They had lost their son. I needed to lounge and just be.

They must have left without my realizing it.

Later, friends were talking about the commotion that had occurred earlier outside. My husband's mother was being forced to come into my parents' home to visit. It was beneath my husband's mother to make the visit, proclaiming that I should have gone to visit her first.

Childhood Friend who had lost her father as a 17-year-old, recalled her paternal grandmother rushing to visit her mother, hugging and crying with her. How in the midst of uncertainty, it made her feel certain that her father's mother had her mother's back.

My friends wondered. *Why didn't your husband's parents hug your kids or show any affection towards them when your kids lovingly approached them? Why was your husband's mother so hostile towards you?* I reminded my friends that everyone has a different way of showing love and that my husband's parents had lost their son.   Let's be empathetic.

Having realized it was important to my husband's mother that I visit her, the four of us got taken to my husband's sister's/their home to pay respects. They seemed happy that we had stopped by. I felt a strange energy in the room-an elephant that I could not see. In my grief, I was still an observer of the life happening around me.

With my kids present my husband's father reemphasized making that trip to Iran. I reassured him that one day we will. We will take that heritage trip to Iran.

I went into the kitchen to see if I could help. My husband's mother talked about the importance of an autopsy to me. How when her Favorite Daughter-in-law's father had passed away they performed an autopsy in Iran. Isn't it law here to perform autopsies? She seemed upset that "I" had chosen not to do an autopsy. She shared her opinion. *Only people who have something to hide do not perform autopsies.* Those words just floated in the air and moved on just as life itself. The visit ended and we pleasantly said our goodbyes.

From the dreadful Friday morning horror, we had ended up at Wednesday morning. It was burial time. Everyone else had managed everything for me. I knew no details. My kids all wanted to leave one item in their father's coffin. So we were driven back home for a split second to pick and bring items. My bedroom horrified me. The mess the paramedics had left behind was a torturous scene.

We got the items required: Manchester United jersey, Stanford cap, and his favorite soccer shorts.

At the funeral home my husband had been prepared for the Muslim burial, nude body cleaned and wrapped with white cotton from head to toe. At my request his face was uncovered for my kids who wanted to say goodbye one last time. It was hard to see his face again at the funeral home and to place his items in the casket. My kids and I were able to kiss him goodbye once again.

He was cold now.
He was still smiling.
He was just cold.
I kissed him on the lips.

I closed my husband's casket.

So many people came. Friends and family spoke at the podium. There was a slideshow of my life in the background. I was an observer and not a participant of this event.

16

I now recall so many who came to me to pay respects. I had appreciated every single person who was there yet it seemed like a movie reel that I was passively watching. It wasn't real. I wasn't really there.

We drove on to the cemetery in a caravan of cars. Somehow I made it to the seating area that was arranged. I sat down and closed my eyes. My husband's mother showed up and requested that I get up to go sit next to her. I did.

There was a lot of chatter around me, not all of which I could understand. A friend was on the ground hugging my knees in an effort to ground my ever shaking. Did my husband's mother ask my friend to stop shaking me?

Was I a prop for a theatrical performance?
Was I not a human shaken to my core for having lost my beloved?

I did not understand my surroundings.
I did not want to understand my surroundings.

I had my pouch.
I had my lavender pouch.
I smelled my lavender pouch.

I had my rosary beads.
I moved with my rosary beads.

As the Muslim prayer and Sufi wisdom came to an end, I opened my eyes to find my kids kneeling by my husband's coffin site. The coffin could no longer be seen. The three of them were throwing rose petals down onto the top of the coffin, into the now open ground. The sight of this broke my heart to no end. I had to close my eyes again for I could not watch anymore.

The next time I opened my eyes the cemetery was empty.

I was taken to my parents' home for a huge dinner my mom had arranged to host all those who attended the funeral. I was not able to eat. Later, I heard about the grandness of the food and set up. I never saw it.

As visitors approached me, I shared personalized moments my husband and I had with them. Though I was in a daze, after 24 years, I had many customized moments to pick from.

My mom and older sister live walking distance apart. I snuck out and went to my older sister's home. I was drained.

I finally was able to sleep some that night, with Tiger by my side. Little did I know that it would take me nine months before I would sleep through an entire night. My older sister's home was full with people sleeping everywhere. I walked around sleeping bodies to find my kids. I wanted to make sure they were breathing. I wanted to make sure they were alive.

I found my younger daughter, my 12-year-old. She was alive. I found my older daughter, my 15-year-old. I could not feel her breath.

I started to scream waking those around her. Help. Help she is not breathing.

My older daughter woke up. *Mom I have a stuffy nose, I'm fine. Go to sleep.*

We all got sick nonstop for months to come.
One cold, flu, and virus after another invaded our bodies.
Lice invaded our hair.
Mice invaded our home.

We were all beat.
We were all broken.
We were all badly bruised.
Would we learn to get back up?
Would there be any light in the midst of our darkness?

Chapter Three
How We Met

The tree had to grow for you and I to meet.

A thousand years begins and ends with you.

I did not want to go out that night.
I was tired.

After university, I was living at home with my parents. My commute to work took over an hour, and I had to be there at 7 a.m. I worked at a strict and old-fashioned engineering firm. Every morning, the president's secretary would walk around the office at 7:05 a.m. to ensure that the engineers were at their desks. She would then make rounds at 3:55 p.m. to ensure the engineers had cleared desks prior to leaving. She was a stickler. In response everyone felt the pressure to be on time.

Pillar Friend called on a Wednesday evening to say she was going to a comedy club with some friends, inviting me to join them.

I had to get up at 5 a.m. to make it to work by 7 a.m. the next morning. I needed my rest. I said No.

My parents were concerned. *Why do you sit at home? You are young. Go out! Have fun!* In their usual fashion, they layered on the guilt, dramatizing their concern about my antisocial tendencies.

By the time I decided to go, I was late to the comedy club. All but one seat was taken and I took that only open seat in the house. Good Looking Guy was seated next to me.

The Comedian talked about how he travels a lot for his work yet sends his wife cards and flowers to remind her that he loves her.

With divine intervention, the Comedian asked me*: Does he send you flowers?* Pointing to the Good Looking Guy next me. I said NO.

Then the Comedian asked Good Looking Guy: *Are the two of you married?*
Good Looking Guy said *Not yet!*

The Comedian went on to explain that if he wanted to marry me he would have to wine and dine me, send me flowers and cards, and make sure I know he loves me. I smiled a polite smile at the Good Looking Guy.

The rest of the night Good Looking Guy and I shared laughs as two do at a comedy show. Once the show ended, I politely said good night to Good Looking Guy. I found Pillar Friend in the crowd to tell her how bummed I was that I didn't get to sit next to her. I loved her for getting me out of the house and laughing.

Saturday morning, I was helping my older sister at her newly opened dental office. My younger sister called. *There is a bouquet of flowers delivered for you and the card says from 'You Know Who.'*

I assured her that I had no idea who would send me flowers. In her jovial manner, she bugged me that I must be hiding a good juicy story from her. As my sisters pressed, it occurred to me that it could be Good Looking Guy from the comedy club. But how would he have my home address?

I called Pillar Friend. Did you give my home address to anyone? She said *Yes, your phone number too.* My reaction was unreal. Are you crazy?

I had had a stalker. A client of the engineering firm I worked for. The odd man had tracked down my home address to connect with me. I had been forced to take stern action to keep him away.

Pillar Friend assured me that Good Looking Guy seemed really nice.

Good looking Guy called the next day to ask if I had gotten his flowers. I thanked him. We talked on the phone and he did seem really nice.

A bit bizarre that he asked me how tall I was. Even more bizarre was that I did not know!!! I don't pay too much attention to trivial matters in life such as how tall I am, how much I weigh, or how old I am. He made a point to tell me he was 5 foot 12 inches.

Silly, I said. Why don't you just say 6 feet tall?

I discovered that apparently a great many do not make the association that 5 feet 12 inches is the same as 6 feet. He later told me that it was in this height exchange that he knew we would be married.

He was blind in love and did overlook my lack of interest in numbers. Over a year later prior to our marriage, his mother asked me how old I was. I got taken aback. I couldn't remember. I figured I could calculate from 1968 to 1993. I got too nervous and I couldn't even calculate. Realizing she had been staring at me and that I hadn't answered yet, I picked a number out of the air to end my torture. I said 28.

Good Looking Guy's mother informed him that I was older than him. Good Looking Guy informed his mother that I'm not. I just can't keep my age straight in my mind.

I recognized that was a negative strike. What kind of a person doesn't even know how old they are?

In our first phone conversation Good Looking Guy was so lovely that I agreed to get together on Friday night. Friday morning, I woke up with a huge headache, throat ache, and any aches you can imagine. I actually made the rare call in sick at work.

That afternoon I called Good Looking Guy to say that I was not able to go out. Later I discovered that he had driven down to my town, a forty-minute drive from where he lived, to find a nice restaurant for the two of us to go to. The days before the Internet....

We spoke on the phone again and I agreed to go to dinner with him the following Tuesday night. Tuesday afternoon, my family was given the amazing news that my older sister was pregnant with her first child and our first baby in my family. We were thrilled and were going to a celebratory dinner. Oh my. I had to cancel once again with Good Looking Guy.

Good Looking Guy called again to say, if I was interested there was a party at his friend's house. I was and said that I would go.

I called Pillar Friend so that we could go together. We did. We entered the party. Pillar Friend saw people she knew and went away to socialize.

I stood there wondering what exactly did he look like? Had I already forgotten? How in the world will I find him in this crowd? I saw a recognizable face that I recalled from the night of the comedy club. Maybe it was him. I went up to say hello. He started talking to me as if we had been friends our entire lives. It felt like he knew who I was. I figured I got it right. It must be him. As life would have it he ended up being Pillar Friend's future husband. He probably knew who I was since he was a good friend of my future husband, the Good Looking Guy. At some point, realizing my level of pure confusion for having mistaken him with Good Looking Guy, he guided me towards his good friend.

I said hello to Good Looking Guy.
I couldn't believe it.
I could clearly see he was there with someone else.
I was cordial.

I exchanged some minor pleasantries in the company of his date. I shortly thereafter said goodbye.

I was looking for Pillar Friend to ask her if we could leave this party and Good Looking Guy appeared right in front of me.

>*I can't believe you actually came.*

I had told you that I would come.

>*Would you like to go out to dinner with me?*

I had told you that I would.

>*But, you made all those excuses about being sick and your sister being pregnant. I thought you didn't want to.*

Those were not excuses. I was truly sick. My sister is truly pregnant.

>*Can I pick you up tomorrow night?*

I prefer not to date guys who already have someone in their lives.

>*I did not come to this party with anyone. I am interested in you.*

Ok- then. I'll see you tomorrow night.

He must have squeezed me into his busy day the next evening. He came. I could hear the rumble of his car from a mile away. He showed up sweaty and in soccer gear. He was setting the scene for the rest of my life. He hadn't had time to go home and shower. I was fine with that.

As Dr. So-and-so's daughter, it was the norm for eligible high caliber "successful" bachelors to come to our home sent by my parents' friends of friends. First they came for my older sister to no avail. She married her own childhood friend. Later it had been my turn.

I had the graciousness of going out on one date. Most would show up dressed to impress. They would bring with them a bouquet of flowers for me. The thoughtful ones would bring two bouquets of flowers, one for my mom too. Most would open the front door of their fancy car and drive me to a fancy restaurant. During dinner, the conversation would be about all their accomplishments.

I had become an expert on ending any hope after a first date.
You are an achieved human being.
You are so accomplished.
You are so this and that.
I am just not ready for a relationship now.
I am sure you will be my biggest regret in life.
I am going through a period of self-discovery.
I would hate to have you miss out on other chances while I discover myself....

All code for "your non-authentic ego is a turn off."

Good Looking Guy had sent his flowers in advance.
He was a complete stranger to my family and me.
His car made a statement that he was three blocks away and approaching.
He showed up sweaty with soccer gear.
It did not occur to him to open the front door of his clunker for me.
The car had papers all over it.
We ended up at a coffee shop where he could fit in wearing soccer clothes. I was overdressed.

Good Looking Guy had a mind at work.
He was brilliant. Yet naïve.
He was generous. Yet broke.
He had a kind being.
He had a pure soul.

We had a heavy conversation about life, religion, souls, and soul mates.

I asked him: Do you believe in soul mates?

He said *Yes*.

And then, with the greatest of convictions, he proclaimed that I was his soul mate.

I was taken aback. I got confused.

How can he be so sure on a first date?

He didn't seem like a player.

He seemed genuine.

In the car ride back home my eye spotted The Twins names that I recognized written on one of the many floating papers in his car.

It turned out that The Twins and Good Looking Guy had done their undergraduate studies in Utah. The Twins had gone to dental school with my older sister, where they had become instant friends.

Twin One was supposed to marry Good Looking Guy's roommate from Utah. Twin Two was marrying her teenage sweetheart, thanks to me as they sweetly recall.

Twin Two had a boyfriend from high school. This relationship had lasted through the long distance college days. And while in dental school, she had decided to break it off with her sweetheart. He was heartbroken.

When dental school ended, Twin Two realized what a mistake she had made. She wanted her sweetheart back to get married to and start a life with. She happened to be visiting Chicago where he was living. Twin Two called her sweetheart to say hello. He was cordial, yet not responsive. Distrusting of her phone call.

—

The Twins had been visiting with my older sister and Twin Two was telling the story of how she had lost the love of her life. He didn't want her back, because he was not being responsive to her.

I interjected into my older sister's conversation with her friends:

Twin Two, did he actually say that he didn't want you back?
  No.
Did you tell him that you loved him?
You were so sorry for breaking his heart?
You want him back in your life, if he would have you?
  No.
So let me get this straight, you called and said hello.
He was non responsive.
Now you assume he no longer wants to talk to you?
  Yes.

Silly Girl.

You have to confess how poorly you had treated him.
You have to confess how remorseful you are.
You have to confess you want a relationship with him, if he would have you back.

I made Twin Two call and beg for forgiveness and proclaim her love. Now they are happily married with two beautiful kids.

The Twins were set to get married on the same night. Twin Two and her teenage sweetheart ended up being the only couple to tie the knot on that night.

I told Good Looking Guy that I was going to Twin Two's wedding. Good Looking Guy said he would have been there too if Twin One was still marrying his old roommate.

At the wedding I told Twin One that I had met a guy that she knew. She looked at me in disbelief.

> *I need to talk to you before the end of the reception.*
> *Make sure you find me before you leave.*

I found her.

> *How long have you known him?*

One date.
Several phone calls.

> *Dump him now.*

Ok?

> *You are too good for him.*

Ok??

> *His entire family is in Iran.*

Ok???

> *He is a player and can't commit.*
> *Changes girlfriends like clothes.*

Got it.
Will dump.

I came back from Los Angeles where the wedding was held.

Good Looking Guy just showed up at my door.
I thought, please don't turn into a stalker.

I was going to dump him on the phone and now he was standing in front of me.

Let's go to a coffee shop.
> *How about an ice cream shop?*

Like a little boy he was so excited to see me.

—

We went to his choice of the ice cream shop. Before I could tell him what I wanted to, he handed me a card. The card proclaimed his love for me.

I have to admit I have never been handed a card proclaiming love on a second date.

I understand you are a player.
We are Soul Mates on our first date.
You Love me on our second date.
You really know how to work it.

> *What are you talking about?*
> *I do love you.*
> *It was love at first sight.*
> *We are meant to be together.*

This is all very lovely.
I spoke to Twin One at the wedding.

I am too good for you.
Your family is in Iran.
You are a player.

It has truly been a treat to meet you.
I think it is best that we end this before it begins.

> *It has already begun for me.*
> *I agree you are too good for me.*
> *My family is in Iran.*
> *I am not a player.*
> *Maybe I was in college.*
> *I am not now.*
> *I am serious.*
> *We are meant to be together.*
> *Why else would the Comedian pick on us in that audience?*

He was so convincing.

He had tears in his eyes.
I wasn't sure what to do.
I gave him a chance.

We went on our third date.
He did seem genuine.
He was very sweet.
Walking by the water he reached to hold my hand.
I was talking about a book I had just read regarding senses.
I asked him to close his eyes.
When one sense is numbed, the other senses are heightened.
He looked so adorable.
I kissed his lips.
He insisted that we had to see each other on Jan. 2nd 1993.
I told him I had plans.
He said he would wake up and meet me at 5 a.m. for breakfast.
I accepted.

On that morning he gave me an anniversary gift.
Our "first month" anniversary.
A book.
A strange book.
IN THE NAME OF GOD, The Khomeini Decade.

He also asked me to marry him.

I just looked at him.
I did not reply.
I changed the subject.

I wasn't sure how to react to a marriage proposal one month
after meeting him at the comedy club, on Dec. 2nd, 1992.

I started to read the book.
What did this mean?
He wanted me to move to Iran with him?

My older sister and her husband got concerned.
What are you reading?

Who are you dating?
Why is he giving you a book about current day Iran?

Let's keep an open mind.
I really had no idea about Iran post-revolution.
I was learning so much.

February 2nd, 1993.
He wanted to make a special date for our "second month" anniversary.
I received another gift.
Another book.
LOVE AND HONOR
Wow. What a drastic difference between this book and the first one.

The books kept coming every month on the second of the month. I realized he wasn't much of a reader. He wasn't giving me the books for their content.

I was so confused.
Fiction. Non-fiction.
The various range of subjects.
I could not solve this puzzle.

It was a puzzle.
The books had a meaning.

In an effort to solve the puzzle, other answers came to me.

It came to me that I had seen Good Looking Guy long before the night of the Comedy Club. He had been at a restaurant on a date. I had been there with Middle School Friend. I recalled his broken arm. Good Looking Guy and I, both recalled our shared moment when our eyes met.

Months later, it came to me that I had seen Good Looking Guy about a year after the restaurant moment at a coffee shop, not realizing he was the restaurant guy. He was talking to his friend about how he felt obligated to go on a date. He just didn't know how to let her down gently. I recalled passing judgment. What a pompous ass thinking he is god's gift to women. He should learn to go home and take a shower after a soccer game instead of going to a coffee shop and stinking the place up.

The answer that came to me was that Good Looking Guy was right. We were meant to be together by the grace of the Divine Universe. The message was sinking in. I believed it too. I also showed him I loved him with my own mind boggler message on the Candlestick Park Scoreboard during a Giants game.

On the ninth month, I deciphered his message.
It came to me.
I solved the puzzle.

I
L
O
V
E
Y
O
U
W

On the tenth month I received a book that started with I.

He continued with the books until he got to Marry Me.

We did.
We got married.
We got married on December 2nd 1994.
We got married 2 years after December 2nd, 1992, the night of the comedy club.

—

We celebrated the 2nd of every month thereafter.
We had agreed to celebrate until December 2nd, 2062.
We last celebrated December 2nd, 2016.
We had been married for 22 years.
We had been together for 24 years.
We had been together for half of my 48 years of life.

What will my next 24 years be?

Chapter Four
Laying Awake

The gathering of people at my parents' and my older sister's homes reminded me of our wedding celebrations.

Did we ever have a wedding? It was a wedding that lasted seven nights of celebration.

Now, my husband had passed away. Every single night has been full of people at my parents' home. His funeral services on Wednesday were followed by a dinner event at my parents' home. Friday was to be his memorial service, with lunch served at the Country Club, hosted by my husband's birth family at their request.

By Friday morning, a week after our dreadful morning, a little bit of mind fog had lifted. I realized that Fashion Friend had been dressing me for these events. I realized that her husband, my husband's cousin, had managed to get a refund for our unused airline tickets to Tehran, Iran.

I also realized that my gums had been heavily bleeding in the past week. Unnaturally bleeding. My older sister, a holistic dentist in addition to being my protector, had taken care of my gums for me on top of everything else. I realized that my younger sister, a chiropractor and naturopath, had been giving me herbs that my body required to maintain emotional balance.

I realized that my kids were around me. I realized Middle School Friend and Pillar Friend taking me for walks. I started to realize how people around me took care of me.

It turned out friends not around me were also taking care of me. Soccer Mom Friend created a future food train to feed my kids and me. Angel Friend, while in India, set up a donation fund for my kids and I. Consider It Done Friend, while in Denmark managed the organization of the creation of a memory book, where friends and family wrote memories they had had with my husband.

We made it to the Country Club for the memorial service very early, and I could not sit. I was too nervous to sit. So I stood on the side of the room by the door, rocking myself comfortably back-and-forth with my rosary beads. Yoga Friend was there to make me laugh in her effort to clean my runny nose. Co-op Friend stood firmly by my side infusing strength energy into my being.

People started to come in. I was there to say hello. I wanted to make sure I showed my gratitude to those who took the time to come. I was standing there the entire time saying hellos and showing my appreciation. I found myself once again sharing moment stories. Mary, my husband loved volunteering in your class. Tibor, my husband loved refereeing for all those soccer games. Ben, my husband enjoyed working with you. At some point, my rosary beads broke.

My husband's mother's youngest sister flew in from Australia with her daughter just in time for the Friday Memorial Service. It was lovely to see them. After 24 years, I had my connections to my husband's extended family. My husband's immediate family had always been suspiciously odd and cold towards me. My husband's maternal grandmother adored me. I adored her. My husband's aunt from Australia is a gem as is the one in Iran. My husband loved his extended family and mine. I learned to love his extended family and appreciate mine more.

I had wanted to leave the hustle of the Bay Area and move to Portland, Oregon prior to having children. My husband refused. Why would we leave your family to move to Portland? I reminded him that they were my family and not his concern. He reminded me that they were also his family and his concern. *We would want them around when we have children.* That was the end of that. Oregon never happened. Our kids grew up making traditions alongside their cousins.

It had not even been two weeks since my husband had passed away. With my focus on my kids, I made my first major decision as an Only Parent. During the holidays, we needed to continue with keeping tradition. I wanted my kids and myself to know that life will continue for us.

It was too late for my sister to have her annual Christmas gathering. However, New Year's was around the corner. New Year's Day we kept the tradition of going to the movies. *La La Land* it was. My foggy brain was in La La Land itself and I couldn't wrap it around the story. I cried for being there without my husband. But first, there was New Year's Eve.

My Hostess Cousin has had a party almost every year for over two decades. Her party got canceled this year as the year her father had passed away.

On December 31st, I called my Hostess Cousin and asked if we could stop by that evening and visit her. I wanted to keep with tradition. I also wanted to visit her and say thank you for all that her husband and she had done in terms of having my back. My Hostess Cousin and her family welcomed us in a very last minute private dinner gathering.

My generous Hostess Cousin had asked if she could invite my husband's family. I asked her to please not. It is not a party. It will be a short evening visit. I explained how my kids and I had planned on sleeping in our own home for the first time since that dreadful morning. We wanted to go to sleep in 2016 and wake up in 2017.

My Hostess Cousin's husband is a God Father in his own right. He plans and brings family together. He is the go to person for advice. Sensing I had not wanted my husband's family around during our New Year's Eve visit, the following weekend he planned a massive breakfast at my home taking care of every detail to include my husband's family. Togetherness in the New Year was the vision.

New Year's Eve was our first night back at my home from having been sleeping at my older sister's home.

We were home by 9 p.m. The four of us were together. The last time we were home was picking up personal items to place in my husband's coffin.

Our home was cold.
Our home was clean.
Our home was somber.

My girls and I decided to sleep together in our master bedroom. We begged my son to bring his sleeping bag and join us in the room. He did only for a few blessed nights. It was so good to have each other. We talked, laughed, and felt safe together. My kids slept.

I lay awake so I could check to make sure they were breathing.
I lay awake thinking.
I lay awake thinking and checking most nights.

I had to do something to start the healing process for my kids. Grief Therapy? I wanted my kids to be rid of their grief yesterday. I was so Naïve. I did not realize this process of trauma and loss will unfold lifelong.

I lay awake in bed with so much to consider.

I wondered how are my kids coping? I realized I am unaware. I wondered how am I coping? I realized I am confused. I wondered how will we survive? I realized I was clueless.

Sleeping together in the same room bonded us on a whole new dimension. My kids and I were all raw and able to share and talk candidly before bedtime.

My kids expressed their gratefulness for still having me, their mother. Losing dad was devastating. Losing mom would be unlivable. My younger daughter shared her fear of losing me. Now that I am all they have, if I die what would become of them?

We formed a new version of our family in this sacred time.

There was wonder. Would it be different if we knew in advance that we would lose dad? If he was sick and we had time to say goodbyes? Would we have been prepared vs. the immense shock we all experienced?

He was gone overnight. There were no real goodbyes. He did not plan anything special for our kids. He did not leave me any instructions for the rest of my life without him. He did not leave words of wisdom for the four of us. He did not show me how his portion of managing our family works. No preparation.

We did love. I guess that could be considered a real goodbye. Lovingly saying good nights. My kids and I were grateful for this.

My younger sister traditionally hosts Thanksgiving. She has a tree structure that she puts out every year and we cut construction paper in shape of leaves and acorns.

Everyone writes what they are grateful for on the leaves and acorns to hang on the Thanksgiving tree. Less than a month before my husband had written he was grateful for his wife, children, and all the sports teams in the Bay Area! I had written one word. Love. I had always been grateful with Love for Love.

I lay awake thinking why gratefulness?
I lay awake thinking what makes life worth living?
I lay awake thinking isn't it easier not to live, rather to live with sufferings?

—

41

I realized I was on a seesaw of emotions.
I realized how lost I was.
I realized how raw I was.
How my heart was a balloon ready to explode.

I was frustrated.
The norm of life was not being respected.
Grandparents are supposed to die first.
Parents are supposed to die next.
Spouses with children should die after they have seen their grandchildren.
Children should never die.

My kids still had both sets of grandparents.
This is unfair.

How can the universe be so cruel and take away my beloved out of the norm of life?

My husband would never be at our kids' graduations.
My husband would never be at our kids' weddings.
My husband would never meet his grandchildren.
My husband would never dance and laugh with us.

I am immensely frustrated at this.
My seesaw of emotions hits me again and again.

Chapter Five
Concussion

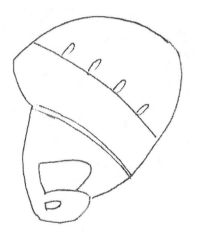

*Sometimes even armor
can't protect us.*

Traumatic Brain Injury. The shock of this unexpected death was so severe it had been the equivalent of my suffering a traumatic brain injury.

Our son had suffered a Brain Injury as a sophomore in high school. YES–Playing Football. This is his recollection of events:

> *I ran the route across the middle of the field, diving for the football spiraling towards me. Eliminating all other distractions from my view, I reached out to grasp the ball, when suddenly my senses went numb. I couldn't feel my body. I was completely blind. All I heard was a buzzing sound and the faint whisper of my coach asking me if I was okay.*
>
> *When I regained consciousness, I found myself surrounded by teammates with concerned looks on their faces. "You all right, man?" my running back asked. "I thought you were dead for a sec." As I racked my brain for memories of what had happened, I realized that I had no recollection of the hit. I felt a rush of fear and wondered just how seriously I was hurt.*

Our son was seriously hurt. Neither coach nor trainer called us regarding this severe injury. Nor did they think about taking him to urgent care. The football coach had shown great interest in our wrestling champion son to recruit him for his football team. He lacked the same interest when our son was injured. Our son just sat out the remainder of the game waiting to be bused back to school.

—

During the fall sports season of his high school freshman year I had thought, what a great sports department. At every practice, there was a 'trainer' to stretch out injuries and provide ice for achy muscles. There was another person for hydration who provided and filled water bottles. Gone were the middle school days when we had to give rides to games. Now there was a bus that picked up both the Junior Varsity and Varsity football teams and transported them as a group to and from their destination near or far. All of this for a football team that had a hard time winning.

Later during the winter sports season, we noticed the stark difference in treatment of Soccer vs. Football. Our son was one of three high school freshmen who made it onto the Varsity soccer team. A winning Varsity soccer team that made it all the way to the Championships. My husband and I couldn't help but notice how there was no trainer on hand, no hydration person, and no buses to transport this winning Varsity Soccer team. My husband would help out by driving our son and some of his soccer teammates to games.

Our son had been an avid soccer player on a competitive team since he was a mere seven years old. Our son's passion for soccer came from his two amazing positive women coaches and my husband/his father who took him to many a World Cup games around the world.

I always did my reminding, as mother would to a child, that he should count his blessings and be grateful for less than 1% of children will get to experience a World Cup game with their fathers at such a young age. Our son couldn't fully comprehend my message at five years old in Germany. However in Brazil, at seventeen, he understood fully. After his father's passing, I know that he will treasure the World Cup memories for his lifetime.

PS- my statistic of less than 1% was my own best guess estimate.

My husband played soccer.
My husband watched soccer.
My husband lived soccer.

My husband was a soccer junkie. He would record European
League Premier games, if he couldn't be up in the middle of
night to watch it live. Then he would not want to listen to any
news nor talk to anyone who would give away the results prior
to him watching the game for himself. Though a Manchester
United fan, he seemed to have enough capacity to watch all
those league games.

I stand corrected. My husband was a ball junkie. Though one
notch down from soccer, my husband felt the same for
football, basketball, and baseball.

Before my husband and I met, I had the privilege of seeing the
Cubs at Wrigley field, the Red Sox's at Fenway park, and the
Giants at Candlestick. After we met, my world of sports
expanded. I attended my first Soccer World Cup, luckily
hosted at home in the United States. I was exposed to the
Warriors, Jazz, as well as many college basketball games. I did
draw the line with the Sharks ice hockey. I had played field
and floor hockey. I just didn't understand or saw a need for
the aggressive behavior of hitting one another during an ice
hockey game. I strongly felt it took away from the honor of the
game. I felt this kind of behavior demeans the crowd by
encouraging the savage cheering for physical fighting. I could
not relate. I chose not to participate.

I started to choose not to be so involved in sports while
allowing my husband his freedom to live his own way. A kind
of live and let live philosophy I have always possessed, which I
realize some have a hard time understanding.

On our second wedding anniversary my husband came home
with a huge childlike smile.

Guess what I got you for our anniversary?

———

I don't know, tell me was my first response.

My husband loved those brainteaser mind games. I was a good sport in playing along.

Is it jewelry? Cold or Hot?
    Cold.
Is it a trip for the two of us?
    Cold.
Is it a kitchen appliance?
    Cold.

Wow, this was going to be hard. If only I knew it was going to be an impossible guess. My husband got 'me' two seats for the Raiders football team in Oakland.

Let me get this straight, you paid top dollar to purchase two seats and then we have to buy all the football game tickets for the season on top of that every year to keep our two seats that you paid for? And you did all this for me, in the name of our anniversary?!

I knew my husband had been on a twelve-year waiting list for 49er season tickets. So when the Raiders came to town, he probably felt as if he had to seize the opportunity.

I went to that first Raiders game with him.
I had never been much of a football fan.

I have to say the cheerleaders bother me. I realize they are physically fit. I realize cheerleaders do not get much credit nor much salary for all the hard work they do to be at that professional level.

It is the feminist in me. Why should a woman jump up and down for a man to play a game? Where are the men who jump up and down for a team of women?

The whole crowd savagely cheering for football players to beat on one another has never done much for me either. The foul language at that first Raiders game, the smell of drugs, and the environment as a whole really got to me.

I told my husband I didn't want to come back to another Raiders game. My husband pleaded with me to give it another chance. My husband could move our tickets to a family section in the stadium where there would be no foul language or drug use. I was infamous for giving more chances in life to all who asked of me. I learned to set boundaries much later in life.

Months later, we went to our second Raiders' game seated in the family section. While a father and son who had clearly done drugs together were loudly yelling using foul language, I turned to my husband to ask if he had really changed our tickets into the family section. The nice man sitting next to me answered for my husband, *Dear, we are in the family section. They just don't do family background checks!*

Football people should do background checks for trainers and coaches. If not, at least give them the know-how that when a high school player faints on the field, they should be transported to urgent care and a parent needs to be contacted immediately.

On that fateful night, our son was bused back to his school where he waited to be picked up by me. My husband was out of town for business. In my exhaustion from work, I had forgotten about the responsibility to pick him up. I had on my nightgown, ready to fall asleep in bed. Our younger daughter came in to ask me where her brother was. I jumped out of bed, thought about changing, and then just grabbed a jacket to wear over my nightgown for the short ride to get our son home from school.

My heart was in my stomach. I noticed that one side of his face had physically dropped. Uneven lips. He had a hard time speaking. His eyes were dilated. I drove straight to urgent care not caring that I was in my sleepwear.

For the first time, I realized what is considered "urgent" at urgent care. In my experience taking my three kids in for the usual broken bones, fevers, and such, a wait of 15 to 30 minutes was typical. That night we did not wait even for one second. We were immediately taken back to a room where the doctor was waiting for us instead!

The doctor asked my son to count backwards from 100.
Our son failed.
The doctor asked our son a simple math addition.
Our math genius of a son failed.
Our son had suffered a traumatic brain injury, better known as a concussion. We had to closely observe him for the next 48 hours to ensure that there would be no internal bleeding. And an appointment was made to visit a neurologist.

It took a total of seven months to recover from two consecutive brain injuries. He was sensitive to light, foggy in his mind, couldn't recall events that had happened that same day, slow in speech, and even sensitive to noise.

I felt the neurologist was useless. All he suggested was rest and time. Mr. Neurologist with all of his education had only one formula: *Let's wait for the headaches to stop. Based on the duration of headaches, the recovery time to go back to sports can be determined.*

The formula was 1:2. If headaches persist for one week, you cannot play sports for two weeks after headaches stop. If headaches persist for two months, you cannot play sports for four months after headaches stop.

Of course our son rested and of course it would take time. It was heart wrenching for me as a mother to not do anything and just wait for things to improve. I felt helpless and useless. I had to learn what I was dealing with so that I would be empowered to ensure proper healing for our son.

I went to work finding alternative therapies.
Here is what I found.
Here is what I did.

Chiropractic.
My younger sister, the Chiropractor, suggested that we wait to ensure we have passed the risk of internal bleeding prior to adjustments. The Chiropractic adjustments helped ensure the blood flow to the various organs in our son's body. A huge help was the adjustment of his jaw to go back into place, balancing his face. The Chiropractor then sent us to the Dentist, my older sister, for the final jaw adjustments that she was so diligently able to do using machinery.

Sleep Study.
Per the Dentist's recommendation, we conducted a sleep study. Our son slept overnight at a special clinic to ensure that there was enough oxygen getting to his brain for healing. It turned out he was not getting enough oxygen to his brain. There was a special CPAP required that our son used every night. I loved this machine, which gave us a report of the level of oxygen he was receiving every night.

Breathing Class.
Realizing how important oxygen is for his brain recovery and life itself, I was able to find a breathing class. A weekend seminar of sorts that our son attended that taught him how to breathe deeply and how to breathe properly.

Acupuncture.
The regular visits to stimulate specific acupuncture points by inserting needles restored the balance of energy through his body, making it possible for him to heal faster.

Nutritional Analysis.
With a combination of Blood tests, Urine tests, Nutritional Response Testing (NRT) and Contact Reflex Analysis (CRA) to assess our son's body, his nutritional weaknesses were found. Then a customized eating plan was created which provided him the recommended vitamins and supplementation necessary to correct these bodily weaknesses. The diet included lots of fatty acids for the brain. The supplementation included fish oils, vitamin C, and more.

Homeopathic.
The Homeopath talked for hours to my son and gave remedies that suited my son's composition to help him heal faster.

Feldenkrais.
The Feldenkrais practitioner worked with my son to ensure ease of movement and awareness of his bones and bodily functions.

Reiki.
As my son lay on a massage table, his aura was infused with positive healing energy.

Massage.
The physical manipulation of our son's body increased his blood and lymph circulation. It also brought him relaxation as well as normalization of his soft tissue.

Aroma Therapy.
I used plant and essential oils to ease any potential depression that may have occurred for our active son who suddenly was not able to be physically active. I had also hoped aromatherapy would speed up his healing process, cure his headaches, and boost his cognitive performance.

And then comes ....

Quantum Healing.

I learned to perform this incredible healing modality on my son. I would have him lay down, close his eyes, and take several deep breaths. Then I would ask a series of questions. After each question asked, I patiently awaited the first answer that popped into his mind.

Where do you feel it in your body?
What shape is it?
What color is it?
How big is it?
Big compared to what?
How much does it weigh?
Weight is equivalent to what?
Take a deep breath.
How would you like to break it into pieces?
With every breath in, "It" is being broken into pieces.
With every breath out, the pieces are being dumped out of the body.

This can be repeated until it becomes harder to locate a tension point in the body.

One day my husband and I were grocery shopping. I must admit doing this activity together was a rare event. We ran into our son's friends' father from elementary school. He asked how our son was doing and we informed him of the concussion. He suggested we contact UCSF Medical Center who had a special program for Teens with Concussions. Our son enrolled in this program that required him to do certain exercises every day for 20 minutes. After a two-month period, his second brain scan showed tremendous improvement in brain activity.

No rock unturned.
I did my ultimate best to turn over any and all rocks for our son.

No rock unturned.

I realized that the trauma of the dreadful mourning had physically injured me. I realized that it was my traumatic brain injury. I realized that just as a person with cancer needs to get help to heal, I too needed help to heal.

I did my best to turn over any and all rocks for my own aching heart, body, and mind.

In the midst of rock turning for our son, the neurologist gave the okay approximately three months after the initial incident for my son to go back to sports. Joy. Our son had decided that he would never go back to playing football. He would only play soccer for his competitive team while wearing a rugby helmet.

His teammates were so excited to have him back on the soccer field. His smile exemplified a joy that I had never witnessed on him. During the first week back at sports on the soccer field, a ball hit his head in the one spot that his rugby helmet did not cover. This caused a whole new concussion, which took four more months of recovery.

At this point, our son suggested that there is a bigger force at play. He is not meant to play competitive sports any longer. This ended his brilliant short-lived sports career.

At this point, I realize that there is a bigger force at play in my life. I am not meant to be with my husband any longer. That dreadful mourning ended my brilliant 24-year companionship.

Chapter Six
Election

Religion of Power.

When my husband passed, it was as if I was living in a different realm.

People moved around me.
Talked to me.
I was just observing.
I wasn't participating.

I was figuratively on my knees.
How could this have happened?
What just happened?
Why did this happen?
Where do I go from here?

My husband proudly took our daughters to the voting poll one month before his passing. He was going to vote for the first woman president of our country and he wanted our girls there to participate in *Herstory.*

Since I was eighteen years old, I have been an avid voter who has rarely missed a local, state, or federal election. I had started to vote by mail when our children were younger.

I could take one child with me to the polls.
With two children, I managed well.
By the time our third child came along, I was having a hard time voting.

Our older daughter made so many phone calls encouraging people to vote for the most qualified individual to run for president in our American history. The candidate happened to be a woman.

The witch (Strong Woman)-hunt was too strong.
The game was dirty.
The real crooks won.

The night of the election, the five of us were invited to several parties. We ended up at my older sister's home with a bottle of champagne to celebrate. As the votes started to come in, we realized we lost Florida, we lost Pennsylvania, and we lost Michigan. There was no return. We went home in shock with the unopened champagne.

We consoled our crying daughters.
It will be okay.
We survived a president who lied and took us to war.
We survived a president who jailed our young men.
We survived a president who took away mental health hospitals and gifted us trickle down economics.
We will survive what is in store for our country.

Our kids finally slept.
My husband and I could not sleep all night.

I walked in circles asking my husband:

How could this have happened?
What just happened?
Why did this happen?
Where do we go from here?

I lived in a different realm that next week. I was in a daze as life happened around me.

Am I living in the same country where people who need it most vote against:

-Fair living wages?
-Affordable health insurance?
-Free vocational schools and training?
-New clean energy industries, meaning: Jobs?
-United States of America and all we stand for?

REALLY?
Did our country in the year 2016 elect a president who:

-Openly assaults women?
-Openly puts down the disabled and minorities?
-Openly commits treason?
-Whose religion is power?
-Whose game is money?

We did. It happened.

So naive I was. What a huge loss this was. I mourned the loss of our first woman president. I mourned that women's rights did not become human rights. I mourned the loss of our first over-qualified president. Listening to Kate McKinnon's *Saturday Night Live* rendition of "Hallelujah" brought tears to my eyes as well as comforted my broken heart.

I had no clue what real loss meant.
I had no clue what was in store for me.
I had no clue that the election was a sampler.

After my dreadful mourning, I danced myself to the end of love for comfort. Leonard Cohen, may he rest in peace, has brought my heart Deep Peace, as has Donovan.

When my husband passed, my thoughts included:

How will my children grow fatherless?
How will I deal with my loneliness?
How can I ever be happy again?

My religion is belief in a higher power.
My game is to live and let live.

Chapter Seven
Financial Abuse

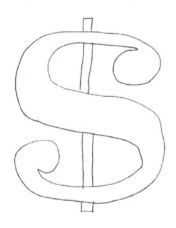

Money=Power=Control
Kindness=Love=Surrender

Money = Kindness
Power = Love
Control = Surrender

Does the need to control, control you?
Do you control the need to control?

My life was out of control.
I was in need of some control.
I had better get started to organize.
I went into my husband's home office and started going through my now papers.

My husband managed the five of us.
My husband managed my parents.
My husband managed his parents.

I pulled out anything that had his parents' name on it to give to his father.
I pulled out anything with my parents' name on it to give to my older sister.

By mistake, I had given my kids' educational funds to my husband's father whose name was on these accounts for tax reasons. My husband had told me about his father's name on our kids' educational accounts. I just hadn't realized what I was handing over because my mind was still foggy.

If someone gave me by mistake something that belonged to them, I would have just returned it.

People are not me.
People are themselves.

I still am learning this life lesson.

People don't think and act like me.
People think and act like themselves.

A couple of days later, my husband's father told me that what I gave him belonged to my kids and it was his son's/my husband's own money that my husband had given to his father to put into those accounts. My husband's father, however, did not return the checkbook. These accounts became a source of explosion.

—

My husband's parents asked me to stop by their place. They were being nice and I had forgotten about the rules for protecting myself.
I thought they needed me.
I went.
My husband's mother, sister, and father were there and started talking about a certain sum of $100,000.

> *Was it in the bank?*
> *When did it arrive in the bank?*
> *It was two payments of $50,000.*
> *When did the payments make it to the bank?*
> *Was it in the accounts now?*

They kept asking.
I kept repeating myself.
I don't know.
I Don't Know.
I DON'T KNOW.
What is this for?

His father mentioned in passing it had been a gift. My husband had told me they had given us a $100,000 gift for our new home but that was almost a year ago.

I was confused. They couldn't possibly be asking about that now. Could it be a different gift? But for what? This sounded like money that had been transferred recently. And my husband, who managed his parents' as well as my parents' accounts, was not around to verify. Why else would they be asking so many questions about it?

I was not an aware person on earth.
I was a floating being in the universe.
I had not wanted to be there.
How stupid of me to have been reeled in by "niceness".

They insisted on an answer.
'I don't know' was not an acceptable answer.

I was unable to get them off my back and stop this
conversation.
I gave the ultimate answer to end the conversation.
I said NO.
NO. There is no such money. Now leave me alone.

As I said No, they proclaimed that I was a liar.
These two $50,000 deposits had in fact arrived.
And my husband had already verified it.

I thought, how dirty.
If you already knew the money had been sent, what was the
need to interrogate me about it?

Did they have an agenda?
Did they need to label me a liar?
Even if achieved by trickery?

Don't they realize they lost their son?
Don't they realize how weak I am now?
Don't they realize it is wrong to attack me?

I had lost my Husband.
I had lost my Rock.
I had lost my Self-confidence.
I had lost my Strength.
I had lost my Senses.
I had lost my Living.

I knew I was weak.

As weak as I was, I was strong enough to realize that I did not
want to be around people who decided they had the right to
frame, interrogate, and accuse me so they could prosecute for
insanity's self-gain.

It felt like I still had my intuition.
My gut feeling was to stay away.
Stay far away from these people with an agenda.

Realistically, can one stay away from family?
I decided to never be alone with them ever again.

How can I forget?
Was I really in this much of a mind fog?
That had been the deal before.

At the start of our marriage, my husband thought it had been
my fault.
His birth family would like me if only I would act differently.
His birth family would like me if only I would do more to win
their hearts.

Then my husband realized it. He saw it. He figured it out.
I was not to be alone with any person from his birth family.
He would always accompany me. We had discovered that they
would not attack me with my husband around.

I was not to give any information to his birth family.
We had discovered that they could not attack me without
information to twist around. He became well aware of their
attacks on me.

The unfortunate side of this coin was the elimination of any
chance for a potential healthy relationship. I believe, in my
being, that we are all connected. We are all here to serve one
another. Why did my husband's birth family feel like a twisted
connection to me?

Now, I am alone.
Now, my husband is not here for protection.
Now, my husband's brother relentlessly approaches me for my
kids and I to travel to Iran.

　　　*An Iran Ski trip? You can buy tickets from this
website.*
NO —They just lost their father and we can not.

　　　A trip to Iran for just the kids without you?

———

66

NO- None of us can travel overseas when we are so distraught.
I prefer not to send my kids to Iran without myself.
Thank you for asking.

> *Tickets to Iran are on sale, what day should I buy your
> tickets for?*

No day. We are not going.

> *Your husband's sister wants to get married. Should I
> buy tickets?*

My best to her. She should move on with her life and get
married. My kids and I will have to be excused from a
wedding in Iran.

> *Your husband's mother is turning 70 next month. I
> looked it up and your kids are off from school for a
> week. I can get tickets for them.*

We wish her the best. 70 years of life is a celebration.
My kids and I are not in a state of mind to be making a trip to
Iran.

My mom noticed my husband's brother's constant badgering
and wanted me to not even think about going to Iran. To
never ever go to Iran with my underage kids. I told my mom
she had nothing to worry about. My husband's family would
never take my kids away from me. They are good people. My
mom made it clear that while I see the good in everyone, they
should have enough wit to not repeatedly ask these questions
at such a time.

The trips in store for my kids and me were visits to the
doctors. I had decided to take all three of my kids to the
doctors to get fully checked out. I wanted to make sure there
was nothing hereditary that could affect them.

My husband's mother and sister insisted on coming to the
doctor when I took my son. I asked my older sister to be there
so that I would not be alone with them.

—

While sitting in the waiting room, my husband's mother mentioned by way of conversation that Islamic law in Iran gives the children to the husband's family after the death of a son. The deceased husband's father has rights to the children. My husband's mother described a Persian movie she had seen where a woman was wailing when the police unwillingly had to take her young children away from her to give them to her father-in-law.

I said the thing about children is that no one really has 'rights' to them. They are living beings in their own right. They are free-living beings in their own right. They do not belong to any person. Respecting a child's being is the most valuable attribute of a society.

As before.
Words spoken.
Meanings not understood.

The bittersweet irony of Islamic law is that the Prophet Mohammed was one of the first known women's rights activists. At a time when women had no rights in the Abrahamic world, the Prophet Mohammed became a voice for change. Mohammed married a woman many years his senior. This was unheard of in those times and still today. Islamic laws were created to protect mothers and children so that they could stay together until the child is able to take care of his own self, which could be interpreted as becoming an adult. Islamic law made it possible for daughters to receive family inheritance at a time when women had no property rights. Islamic law made it possible for women to get a divorce and obtain property during a divorce. Our common property law in California has its roots in Islamic law via Spain. The interpretations, by men, of Islamic law seem so demeaning to women in today's time.

I changed the conversation from children being property to how I wanted to make sure that my kids would survive the devastating loss of their father. I am looking at everything I can do for them: doctor visits for their health, grief counseling, keeping with family traditions, and not changing their lives in any way.

Out of the blue, my husband's mother goes on to explain Islamic inheritance law to my older sister and me. When a son who has a family dies, his own birth family inheritance is not passed on to his children. His descendants get erased from the equation.

I wanted to say, Lady why are you telling me these things?
I wanted to say, Lady I can't wrap my head around money.
I wanted to say, my husband died. Your son. Don't you get it?
I wanted to say, I don't recall asking for my kids to get inheritance from you.
I really wanted to say, you can shove your money up your ass.

Instead, I kept face.
I said, in the United States, it is up to the individual to make inheritance decisions. However, not everyone is capable of making such a decision.

Once Again.
Words spoken.
Meanings not understood.

My older sister looked at me with disbelief.
She later asked me:
> Does your husband's mother always speak in
> parables?
> Is she making this stuff up?

My husband's birth family had made an appointment with my husband's doctor to find out WHY my husband had died.

I did not want to go.

Again, what has happened has happened.

Are we ever capable of answering the 'Whys' of life?

Especially medical doctors, they are just ordinary people who make mistakes every day. My dad made sure I knew that medical doctors don't have all the answers. My dad was a sought after surgeon in his younger days. Too much faith and importance is placed on this profession that is marched on by ordinary people who have to act like gods.

I thought I should go.

I should be there.

I did not want to be alone with them.

Pillar Friend came by and took me to this all-hands meeting.

We were late. We walked in.

The conference room of the medical office had a long oval table and chairs.

Callous Doctor and Research Doctor were seated on one side. My husband's father, mother, sister, and brother seated on the other side.

Pillar Friend recorded the meeting.

She had indicated that because of my state of mind, I would not be able to wrap my mind around this matter. Her recording was for a future possibility that I would want to revisit this information.

My husband's birth family was asking questions and the doctors were answering.

Do I come from a different world that sees my husband's passing as God's will?

I get it. Your son died. You are looking for answers.

I empathize. I do.

But it is what it is.

Nothing I do will bring my husband back.
No one can tell me WHY it happened.

Conclusion of the meeting:

The upshot of the meeting was that the doctors should have detected that there was something seriously wrong with my husband's heart. He had gone in for a test at prestigious Stanford Hospital. Research Doctor probed into his heart and felt there was not a need to place a defibrillator, as everything looked functional. The doctor recommended medication and monitoring. It turned out that a defibrillator may have saved his life.

Monitor is code for Research. A personality type of researcher should be in a lab monitoring and researching. A personality type of problem solver should be in working with patients face-to-face to solve issues. When research doctors don't realize where they belong, tragedies arise.

Research Doctor had enough wit to say that she had learned a lesson from my husband's death. She will be more assertive with other patients in the future.

The doctors leave and give us the conference room.
Now without any doctors in the conference room, the attacks began.

First attack.
   Why didn't you have him change doctors?

I justified myself and explained how the answer is not with the doctors. I took care of my family. I provided health by consciously eating local organically grown earth foods. I understood that wellbeing is from the inside out. I taught my husband the importance of drinking water and deep breathing. I had my husband visit a holistic doctor who had detected weak points in his body. I could not force him to care. I could not force him to change doctors. He was his own person. He made his own decisions.

Second attack.
> *You didn't perform an autopsy. You are so cheap, you didn't want to pay out of pocket to do an autopsy. How dare you not perform an autopsy to find out why this happened and what time exactly it happened?*

Again I justified and explained that an autopsy does not give you an exact time of death to the second. Someone somewhere already explained to me that the electrical part of his heart did not send a signal.
I did not see a need to cut my husband up if there was no benefit for my kids. He is gone. Nothing and No one can bring him back.

Pillar Friend stepped in to inform my husband's family that my son did not wish to do an autopsy. He did not want his father cut to pieces for science.

Third attack.
> *What kind of a mother listens to and has her seventeen-year-old make decisions? Seventeen-year-olds are not capable of making such decisions.*

I was tired of their attacks.
I was tired of responding and justifying myself to them.

These conversations were loud.
Medical personnel came and asked us to leave the conference room.

We walked outside to the waiting area.

This is a moment where I stooped low by association.
Feeling under attack, I felt justified in throwing a real attack
their way.

I asked my husband's parents, What happened last night?

I just don't have attacks down like they do.
It doesn't come naturally to me.
It is not my game to participate in.
My attack question didn't go over the way I anticipated.

The night before I had been waiting for them to come and
spend time with my kids. They had called and I told them we
would be home if they'd like to stop by. They agreed that they
would come.

Instead of justifying why they didn't show up to see my kids,
their own grandchildren, they turned that around to be my
fault too! Wow, these predators sure know how to attack.

When will I learn?
People do not act and think like I do.
People think and act like themselves.

Fourth Attack.
 You were supposed to call us back to verify.

What? Why would I call you? We had already spoken. I told
you we are at home and my kids would love to spend time with
you. What was not verified?

Drained.
Speechless.

Their loss.
They didn't want to spend quality time with their own
grandchildren.

At the request of the medical personnel who were now asking us to leave the waiting room, Pillar Friend and I said goodbye and walked away.

Pillar Friend was in shock after having witnessed the abuse I had endured by these people.

I was in shock. They were abusive to me in front of "other" people. Typically, in front of people, they wanted to show off our relationship as loving and close. The fake, *sit next me* and let me tell you jokes to make you laugh. Everyone should think how wonderful we are towards you. The abuse was always when they found me alone. They hadn't been able to be alone with me for so long and they just couldn't hold it in any longer.

Pillar Friend hugged me in the car and asked me how I was holding up. She could not believe their behavior.

I explained them away.
They have just lost their son and brother.
They feel angry.
They don't have healthy means of dealing with their emotions.
They are taking it out on me.
Don't worry about me. I'll be fine.

Pillar Friend knew better.
She had been in my life for all of my marriage.
She had known about them from my past.

Pillar Friend drove me home.
The next thing we knew, they stopped by my home as well.
They are mother, father, and brother.
Pillar Friend saw them in.
Made them tea.
And kept a conversation with them.

In an effort to bring positivity, I shared how my husband, their brother and son, lived a life of love. How he knew he was loved. I would tell him everyday. I would tell him how grateful I was that he was in my life.

My husband's father shared his opinion. *Only conniving people will verbalize love and gratitude in an effort to trick for self gain.*

What was I to do with that?
Are you suggesting that I'm conniving?
Are you projecting because you are conniving?
Are you in pain because your wife may have been conniving?
Are you in pain because your wife may have never told you she loves you?

I am confused at the depth of his statement.
I understood that it was meant to be an attack on me.
My heart sent loving energy to his paranoiac mind.

They kept hinting that they needed to talk to me alone.
Pillar Friend did not budge. She would not leave me alone with them. They finally gave up and said their goodbyes.

To this day, I'm grateful for Pillar Friend.
I'm grateful that she had the fortitude to have my back.

I will refer to my husband's birth family and Favorite Daughter-in-law as the Herd. The Herd was going on a trip to Pismo Beach. My husband's mother invited my kids and me. I explained that I didn't have the bandwidth for a trip. It hadn't even been a month since my husband's passing. My kids had activities such as soccer games and theatrical performances. I wanted normalcy for my kids' lives.

Truth be told, I didn't want to be alone with them for one minute.

—

75

Why would I put myself in a situation of being alone with them for an extended amount of time, trapped in the same lodging in a different town?

Not being able to get me alone became a clear point of frustration for my husband's parents. My husband's mother lovingly called me to ask if they could talk to me alone.

I told her, I am afraid of you.
I do not wish to be alone with any of you.

She said she had purchased two books for me while in Pismo Beach. She insisted that there was nothing to be afraid of. They wanted to help me and we needed to get together for them to see what they could do to help. I wasn't falling for any more lies. Offering a child candy to lure them into Hell.

This is how they have operated.
Be mean.
Realize you have lost me.
Be nice to reel me in only to be mean again.

I stood my ground.
If you have something to say to me, you can say it in front of other people.

It became the most unbelievable turn of events.
It was like we were preparing for a boxing match.
Phone calls back and forth.
Setting up a time to meet.
Setting up a place to meet.
Setting up their family meeting.
Setting up who would be present at this all hands-on-deck meeting.

I asked my sisters to join me. I wanted to spare my mom and dad. My sisters' asked their husbands to join. My Tribe came to pick me up. We went with pastries that my younger sister had brought.

My husband's father, mother, sister, and brother saw us in. Pleasantries were exchanged. We all sat around in a circle, on chairs and the ground, in the living room.
My husband's father started to speak.

1.

> *Your son's educational account has X dollars and Y cents, your older daughter has $A and B cents, and your younger daughter has $R dollars and S cents. You clearly do not need any help with their college expenses.*

My older sister explained that college is not just tuition. There are a lot of expenses such as travel costs, living expenses, etc. Also, we cannot know how much is too much or too little. It all depends on what college they will attend and if there will be a scholarship or not.

My husband's father suggested that there should be an account opened into which that my dad puts money and my husband's father will match for any extra educational expenses. My husband's father also suggested that he will have the executive power of this account for my kids' college spending.

I know my sisters were floored at this statement.

2.

> *There is the matter of the $100,000 that must be returned. It was a gift meant for our son, not his lying wife who was trying to hide the receipt of this money from us. If it is not returned, every penny needs to be accounted for. You have to provide expenses against this money to us.*

My older sister in a comically polite way suggested that the person who can resolve their concerns lies at the cemetery.

—

I, on the other hand, am a pleaser and justifier. I said that my husband was an excellent record keeper and I can surely bring this matter to a resolution for them.

3.

> *There is $70,000 that your husband owed us. You will not find any record of this in any bank statements or anywhere for that matter. You now carry this debt.*

My mind is blowing at this point. Is this money you spent on raising your child? Do I owe you for that? My husband, the record keeper, didn't keep a record of this? Do you know how hard it is to bring money from Iran? Of course there would be records.

This is not at all what I had expected. What happened to we need to talk to see what you need and how we can help?

My sisters and their husbands were stunted. They tried to keep face for me.

4.
There is the apartment that was purchased in Tehran, Iran, 20 years ago by my husband and I. This apartment had haunted my in-law relationship for the majority of my marriage. My husband's father gave us a lesson on Islamic law.

> *Islamic law dictates that when a man dies, his property is divided into units. The deceased's parents receive 2 units, when still alive. The deceased's son/s will receive 2 units. The deceased's daughter/s will receive 1 unit. The wife gets nothing.*

However, due to the generosity of my husband's parents, they will not take their 2 units and would leave it for their grandchildren.

My husband's father goes on to explain that 20 years ago, my husband and I sent $60,000 to Iran for this apartment. They spent $20,000 of their own money for us to make this deal happen. The apartment is now worth $180,000.

Wow- I thought, you waited for 20 years to pass and my husband to pass to tell me that I owe you $20,000 for real estate that per Islamic law doesn't even belong to me anymore.

My sisters were thinking why I never told them that I had bought an apartment in Tehran, Iran.

My husband's mother speaks. She mentions that a deceased's sale of property in Iran is problematic and long. Since her husband has a power of attorney from his son, my husband, he should just sell the apartment now and not worry about going through the declaration of death. My younger sister and her husband see her point and defend her against her husband who adamantly says no to her. He will do things legally.

Everyone forgot that I should be the decision maker for the apartment being sold or not and I had not made a decision. It ends.

5.
My husband 's father hits his last point. He wanted the tombstone to be written in Persian. He wanted my husband's last name to be written as the full Persian name instead of the shortened American version.

My younger sister's husband told of his experience creating a tombstone for his father. We all agreed that of course we would honor my husband's father's request.

As my husband's father concluded this meeting, he asked if we had any concerns.

My older sister's husband spoke about the matter of ensuring that the kids and I, their widowed mother, survive financially in the critical initial year. *Are you willing to help out with any potential necessary living expenses of your son's family?*

Wow.
Was that ever the asked question?
Was that ever the question not to ask?
Was that ever the exchange?
Of course the answer was NO.

My husband's father made it clear that I have a business and make money, therefore should handle my life with my kids just fine.

My older sister explained that living expenses in our area are very high, not to mention having three children with activities such as competitive soccer and theatrical arts.

My husband's brother stepped in to confirm that living expenses are high in this area. Then lunged right in to ask my older sister's husband how much cash I have in my bank accounts.

I was taken aback.
Why was he asking him instead of me?
Why was he asking at all?

My older sister's husband was taken aback too.
He said he had no clue how much money is in my accounts.
He truly did not.
How would he know what my bank accounts hold?

After all, my husband's birth family had more of my financial details that they so openly shared today with my sisters.

My husband's brother accused my older sister's husband of lying. *You know how much money she has and you don't want to tell us.*

———

80

It started occurring to me.

They all went to the brokerage firm to see how much money I had in my kids' educational accounts to the cent. They must think that others behave in the same manner, given an opportunity.

My husband's sister chimed in attacking my older sister's husband. *You called my parents' accountant to see how much money they make.*

My older sister's husband went into justification mode. Since your brother's passing, I'm taking care of my father-in-law's books. Your brother used the same accountant for our father-in-law that he did for his own father. Why would I even care how much money you make? Also, this is the United States of America no accountant would give personal information to someone else. And as Americans, we respect privacy and don't even think of wanting to know other people's personal information.

My husband's father turned the conversation back to *she makes enough money with her business to run her household and take care of her children. Period.*

Everyone got up to say goodbyes. My Tribe just wanted to leave. Keeping face, we all thanked them for hosting the meeting. We pleasantly said our goodbyes and left.

As soon as we left, my younger sister hugged me.
> *I had no idea this is what you had to deal with all these years.*
> *You sure shouldn't have to deal with it now.*
> *I'm so sorry.*
> *How draining.*
> *I'm here for you.*

My older sister shared her thoughts on how they want to steal your apartment in Tehran, Iran. Did you notice how you conveniently now owe them $190,000 when your apartment, that per Islamic Law is not even yours, is supposedly only $180,000 in the expensive heart of Tehran, a city that compares to Manhattan in pricing?

I told my older sister that my husband's parents are good people. They are very well off and would never steal from their own grandchildren.

My older sister then revealed something else that she had not shared earlier out of a desire to protect me. In the first week after my husband had passed, our parents took care of what needed to be taken care of. My husband's sister insisted that my husband's birth family take care of the Friday memorial service. They did.

Afterwards my husband's sister came to my older sister wanting a refund of $16,000 from the Estate of her brother for the expenses of the Friday memorial service. My older sister explained to her that there is no 'Estate'. The estate is me and my three now fatherless children. My older sister explained that not wanting to put pressure on the four of us, knowing that my husband our main breadwinner was lost, my parents were taking care of the funeral expenses.

My husband's sister made the suggestion to share the bills. My older sister thinking she is talking about all the bills for all the funeral services said there is no need. My husband's sister returned to request that they be paid $8,000 –half of the Friday memorial service fees.

My older sister was stunned at this request. No one had asked them to spend the money for the Friday memorial service. Now that they have spent the money, first they want a refund from a widow and her children. Then they ask for a half refund from me. My sister rolled up her sleeves. She went back presenting them with receipts of all that was spent saying if you want to "share", you owe me $5,000 on top of the $16,000 that you spent. At this point my husband's sister dropped the subject. No money was exchanged.

My older sister went on to warn me to be careful. *They are predators. You need to stand up for yourself. Stop trying to be so accommodating. Stop justifying yourself to them.*

I reminded my sisters and their husbands that they have lost their son and brother. They are generous people. They are good people. I'm sure they are not in a right state of mind.

The conversation turned to how people show their true nature in a crisis.

We then all laughed about the worst investment in the world. Pay $60,000 and 20 plus years later you have to pay another $20,000 for something supposedly worth $180,000 in a country that you can't even get your money out of.

Money. Money. Money.

All this talk about Money.
I started thinking, how will I take care of my kids?

Like moving uphill with an elephant on my back, I attempted to get organized with money.

First easy thing first.

Before my husband's parents go back to Iran, I needed to transfer my kids' educational accounts to my name.

I asked my husband's father to please come with me to the brokerage firm to handle this.

My husband's father and sister came with me.

Prior to going to the firm, I went on the firm's website and prepared the necessary papers to transfer the educational accounts into my name. I wanted to spend the least amount of time with them at the brokerage firm.

The fact that I had prepared papers irritated my husband's sister. She made the comment that I look like a lawyer. Really? Filling out an application online is emulating a lawyer?

The brokerage firm 'consultant' was so talkative.
The consultant wanted me to know that if my kids' accounts are in my name and my income level was high, I would not be able to contribute as much to my kids' educational funds.

I kept repeating that my husband took care of our finances. I'm not sure of our income. I want the educational accounts in my name. I may or may not decide to contribute in the future. My husband's sister wanted to know the exact number of my annual income prior to 'approving' the account transfer.

Numbers?
My annual income?
Seriously?

I don't know. I especially freeze and don't know when there is an imaginary answer gun pointed to my head.

Could it be that my husband's sister also had many life lessons to embrace?

That other people don't think the same as her.
That other people don't act the same as her.

Not everyone is a number junkie.
Not everyone pays attention to numbers.

The fact that I did not know my annual income further irritated my husband's sister.

The transfer did not happen.

What did happen in that meeting was that I realized that they had met with this consultant before and in person.

Did that feel dirty to me?
Yes.

It is two nights before my husband's parents are going back to Iran. They invited my kids and me out to dinner. I took my dad with me so as to not be alone.

I asked my husband's father, in front of my dad, to please let's go back to the brokerage firm and convert my kids' educational accounts to my name. Life is unexpected. What if something happens? You are in Iran and the political climate is volatile. My husband's father agreed. We planned on going to the brokerage firm the next day.

In the morning of the next day, prior to our appointment, my husband's father called.

I will not meet you at the brokerage firm.
I have thought it over and I will not transfer the children's money into your name.

Did I hear correctly?
My money that my husband and I placed in these accounts for our kids, you do not wish to transfer into my name?

> *You cannot be trusted with the financial well-being of your children. I am not entrusting you with their college money.*

I will leave signed checks and checkbook with my son.
You take proof to him of any expenses you have and he
will write you a check.

Please listen to your heart.
Please listen to what you are saying.

Is your heart sure this is what you want to say to me?
Is your heart sure this is how you want to treat me?
Is your heart sure this is Godly?

> *My heart is sure this is what I want to say to you.*

Then my husband's sister grabbed the phone and came on the
line.

> *STOP dis-respecting my father.*
> *We have made our decision.*
> *You are not trustworthy.*
> *You are not capable.*
> *We will not make the transfer.*

I hung up on her.
I started to shake.
I started to cry.
I was beside myself.

I had been the wife of their son for 22 years.
I am the mother of their three grandchildren.
Let's assume I'm the most Evil person to walk our earth.
What is rightfully mine should still be mine.

How dare they.
How dare they treat me in this manner.
How dare they accuse me of traits I do not possess.
I am capable.
I am officially Silicon Valley Woman Entrepreneur of the Year.
I am unofficially an amazing conscientious mom for raising
self-reliant and self-sustaining children.

How dare they.

I am trustworthy.
I am trustworthy to all who know me and of me.
I am the one who always says it like it is.
My husband trusted me with his life, our three children.

How dare they.

My own father is not typical of the Iranian older generation.
I called my husband's father's friend.
I wanted a true Iranian older generation perspective.
I wanted to know if it is cultural to treat a daughter-in-law in this manner?
I wanted to know if it is cultural to think of monies as belonging to their son only?
I wanted to know if it is cultural to suggest that the brother-in-law will now handle my kids' finances?
I wanted to know if I am misunderstanding a bigger cultural picture?

Did my broken heart want to shame slap?

He doesn't really get what I'm asking...
He wanted to know how much money is in the accounts.
He wanted to reassure me they are well off.
He wanted to reassure me that they would never take my money.

Again.
Words spoken.
Meanings not understood.

Though my mind was confused my heart had always known the reason for the Herd's treatment of me. They believe that they are intellectuals and are terrified of mystic me. They operate from their inflated egos and fear.

Their belief as intellectuals knows not the faith of heart.
They are fearful of my faith.
They are devoid of faith.

I had believed it was not about money.
Money was their gun to shoot me with.
Money was their language to show me with.

Show me I did not belong with them.
Show me I was not loved by them.
Show me I, the mystic, was never welcomed in their lives.

My husband's father's friend was kind enough to give me an offer. He wanted me to know that he would personally make sure these monies are returned. He wanted me to let it go until my husband's parents returned from Iran in a couple of months.

I do.
I tried to let it go.
I tried to give it to Jesus.
Could I really let it go?
Not at the time. No. Not really.

Was their action the last straw on my camelic back?
No. Not yet.

The evening of the day I hung up the phone on my husband's sister and the night before my husband's parents left for Iran, my husband's sister had the audacity to show up at my door.

I opened the door reluctantly and asked her what she needs.
She said she had come to see 'our' kids.
I asked her to come in.
I asked my kids to come downstairs to spend time with their aunt.

I was cleaning dishes in the kitchen.
Ignoring her.
She came over to make conversation with me.
I was cordial.
I was cold.
I was cordial.

She said goodbye and left.

I called my older sister.
I told her about my day.
I told her my husband's sister stopped by.
I told her I don't want to be alone.
I told her I don't feel safe.

She told me she is shopping.
She would stop by to be with us later.
My nephew stopped by to help my older daughter with her
Chemistry.

My nephew and my girls went upstairs to study on our now
family bed.
My son was out with his friends.
I was now in my sleepwear ready to hop into my daughter's
bed to sleep.
Someone was at the door.
I thought it was my older sister and her husband checking in
on us.
I quickly changed and ran downstairs.
I opened the door.
It was my husband's father and sister.

They came in.
My husband's father didn't even ask about my kids.
He is going to Iran the next day and he didn't even care to see
my kids.
In a derogatory tone, he asked me for my husband's Iranian
passport.

Thank God I didn't have our passports at home.
I didn't have any documents at home purposefully.

I told him that I didn't have it.
What do you need it for?
I can try to get it to you before your flight in the morning.
He said he needed it to get an Iranian death certificate for his
son.
I reassured him that I would try to make it happen before his
flight.

Then he went on in that same derogatory tone to say he has
brought my checkbook. *Now tell me, how much money you
want and what you want it for. I will write you a check
tonight.*

I stopped him.
I don't need any money from those accounts.
>*I will leave signed checks and checkbook with my son.
You can show him proof of what money you need and
he will write you a check.*

I need you to do the right thing and leave the checkbook with
me.
I need you to do the right thing and transfer my kids' accounts
to me.

>*Your husband didn't trust you.
Why do you think those accounts are in my name and
not yours?*

Seriously, are we going to no man's land again?
For tax reasons! It was for tax reasons.
That is why they are in your name and not mine nor his.
He trusted himself and they are not in his name.
We made too much money to put away the maximum for our
kids tax-free.
My husband found a legal loophole. Putting your name on our
kids' accounts allowed us to save more money for our kids.

It has nothing to do with my husband's trust of me.
My husband trusted me with our treasures, our children.
My husband trusted me with our finances.
My husband trusted me. Period.

My husband's sister steps in.
> *STOP dis-respecting my father.*

> *You are untrustworthy.*
> *The money in those accounts and this home you live in*
> *is what my brother worked for and it is not yours. We*
> *don't know what you want to do with my brother's*
> *money. You can just take off with the money and*
> *leave your children hanging.*

Money. Money. Money.
Seriously.

I'm thinking please older sister come.
Please come as soon as you can.
Please be here.
Somebody.
I can't be alone with these people.

My girls were upstairs.
My nephew was upstairs.

I said to my husband's father, imagine your future son-in-law's
family treats your daughter the way you all are treating me. Is
this Godly? Would you want this for your own daughter?

My husband's Godless sister steps in.
> *STOP dis-respecting my father.*

Of course, you can't understand that the money your brother made in over two decades that we were married belongs to my kids and me. You can't understand, because you did not build a life like we had. News alert for you- we made our lives outside of your family influence. My husband was not a trust fund child like you and your brother.

Would you want your future husband's family to treat you the way you are treating me?

Well, I am not You.

Did she just say:
I am not You?
I am Not you?
Did she just fucking say I AM NOT YOU?

Does she believe that she is somehow superior to me?

Doesn't she know that an exterior look that society craves does not equate to worth.
Doesn't she know that having degrees from prestigious universities does not equate to worth.
Doesn't she know that the clothes one wears and the car one drives does not equate to worth.

Is she so engrossed in her own ego?
Doesn't she know worth comes from one's heart?

Meanwhile, my older sister had walked in with her husband and had witnessed this exchange.

I started yelling.
Did you hear what she said?
Did you hear her?

What the heck am I going to do with money my husband and I have spent years saving for our kids?
Where do they think I'm going to take off to?

———

What do they think I'm going to spend my own money on? Who do they think they are coming into my home and telling me I'm untrustworthy?

My husband's sister throws out her proof.
> *You lied to us about the $100,000.*
> *You told us it was never received.*

WHAT?
The one you wouldn't take 'I don't know' for an answer during your interrogation only two weeks after my husband had passed, despite the fact that you already had an answer because my husband had verified it with you in the past year.

How dare you.

I had had enough.
I left.
I went to go upstairs.

As I was climbing up the stairs I could hear my husband's sister telling my older sister everything is not about the wife, they have had a loss too.

My older sister was saying that this is not a competition. *We are all heartbroken and we have all had a major loss. I have also lost a brother in him. It is your brother's wife and her children that are most affected by this tragedy. They are the ones needing our support.*

As I make it up the stairs, I think, is my husband's sister crying for help? It still gives her no right to attack me.

I could hear my older sister telling my husband's sister attacking me was not a smart move. If they wanted the children in their lives, they needed to stop attacking the children's mother. I hear my husband's sister aggressively asking my older sister, *are you threatening me with our own children?*

Was she thinking that my husband's family could attack me, disregard my being, and still my children would flock to my husband's family by free will?

In Iran, there is a law that rips dependent children from their mothers as my husband's mother had educated me. Did my husband's sister not realize there is no such law in the United States?

In researching historical sites to visit for our heritage trip to Iran, advisory warnings from the State Department kept popping up on my computer screen. Travel to Iran at your own risk. Oh my God, had that dreadful morning in the United States been a dreadful evening in Iran, what would have been of my life? Could I have been stuck in a foreign country and my kids taken away?

Conversations downstairs were so loud that my girls, nephew, and I could hear them from upstairs. The girls were terrified.

We could hear my older sister's husband trying to calm them.
>*I have had loss.*
>*I lost my sister in an unexpected car accident when she was 24 years old.*
>*I lost my mother at the young age of 64 during a minor medical treatment.*
>*I can empathize with you.*
>*It is hard to live through loss.*

My husband's father saying *that we need to control her finances because she is not capable and not trustworthy. She comes from a family of untrustworthy people shown by her younger sister and that husband of hers suggesting that I illegally sell the apartment in Iran.*

My older sister's husband saying *your wife made the suggestion and if younger sister and her husband defended your wife, they were wrong. You are right.*

Regardless, she is capable. She is trustworthy. She can handle her own finances. Why would she run off with her own money? Her children are her life. They are all she has left. Where would she go? What are you suggesting?
My girls were hugging me at this point.
My younger daughter acknowledged, *I thought it was only dad's mother that was mean to you Mom.*

A thought crossed my mind. How will my kids reconcile their relationship with their father's family after witnessing this heinous behavior towards their mother?

I asked the girls, as hard as it has been, please try to concentrate on your homework and learning Chemistry.

I needed to lay down.
I needed quiet.
I left my girls and nephew on our family bed.
I went into my younger daughter's room.
I collapsed on her bed.

I heard my husband's brother's voice downstairs.
He was downstairs?
My God.
Why in the world is he here?
When will this end?

My mind took me to my own brother.
In a moment of vulnerability, he had shared how he took a severe beating from his own high school football teammates at the age of 15 due to being Iranian American in the time of the hostage crisis. The coach did nothing. I recalled believing that my brother had been injured in football. Badly injured with broken bones and that knee.

That was then and now is not much different. At my older daughter's advanced high school that has gender friendly bathrooms, predators made a *Nigger Kill List*. One of the victims had to leave school for safety reasons. These predators still roam the school halls now demeaning smart girls.

I had been ostracized as a ten-year-old during the same hostage crisis era my brother took a beating. I healed my adult self by going back to my ten-year-old self and empowering her.

I asked my brother, what would your adult self now say to that fifteen-year-old boy? What would you wish he had done?

He replied, *stand up for myself.*
File a complaint to my school administration.
Go to the news media.

No Shame. I am NOT at fault.
No Guilt. It was NOT my fault.

Then I heard my husband's brother downstairs saying the $100,000 is our money and she needs to return it to us.

The one person in the Herd who had never attacked me to my face was now attacking me behind my back. The one person I had hoped would have courage and not be a bystander of abusive behavior towards me was now abusing me.

God knows how many hundreds of thousands of dollars had been gifted to this trust fund son and his wife to show favoritism. One freaking gift of $100,000 in 22 years of marriage is not digestible?

This became the last straw on my *camelic* back.

I lost it.
I lost it for my husband.
I lost it for myself.
I lost it for all those who have ever been attacked.

I ran downstairs.
I yelled.
I yelled as loud as I could.
I yelled, joined by the voices of all humans who have ever taken a beating.
I yelled with my lungs, then my diaphragm.
I yelled, GET OUT –GET OUT

Husband's Brother, I have to come and ask your permission to spend my own money?
GET OUT

Husband's Sister, the $100,000? One day my husband stole it, the next day it was a gift that I must return? And I'm the untrustworthy one?
GET OUT
GET OUT
GET OUT
GET OUT
GET OUT
GET OUT

I kicked them all out.
My older sister and her husband included.
I shut the door behind them.
Went upstairs.

My girls were wide eyed looking at me.
        Are you okay mom?
I'm fine.
NO, I'm great.
Actually, I haven't felt this fantastic in years.

I feel released.
I feel free.
I feel sane.

        Why did you yell like you did?

———

Because I can't take it anymore.
Because I won't allow it anymore.
Because I am done with it.
Because I yelled the way I did, they have to think twice before
throwing garbage our way ever again.

My older sister called me to ask if I was okay.
I told her I'm fantastic.
Best I have been since my beloved passed.

The next day I was up early and called the Interests Section of
Iran in Washington DC. I learned that my husband's passport
didn't need to go to Iran to get an Iranian death certificate.
I am able, very able, to take care of an Iranian death certificate
in the United States of America. It also helps that I have
strong family connections willing to take care of this task for
me.

I called my husband's parents.
I wished them a safe journey.
My husband's mother was being very nice to me.
I didn't care.
It was too little, way too late.
Only God knows if she was just being nice to reel me in again.
It didn't matter to me anymore.
I had had enough.
I finally reached my limit.
I was done.

I told my husband's father, I will not give you my husband's
passport. I will get an Iranian death certificate myself.

He told me I'm not capable.
I reassured him I was quite capable.
I also told him, as my husband's parents and my children's
grandparents, I will deal with the two of them only.
I will not be dealing any longer with my husband's siblings.

Like a child trying to one-up another, he then said he would deal with me only. He will not be dealing with my older sister and her husband.

While I stood by our agreement, it wouldn't take long for my husband's father to forget his end of this agreement.

Ciao.
Adios.
Auf Wiedersehen.
Shalom.
Wadaeaan.
Totsiens.
Zaijian.
Good-Bye.

Khoda Hafez.
My God protect me.
May God protect you.

Chapter Eight
Dreams

My heart feels the hurt of pain.
My heart knows the strength to withstand.

I couldn't sleep at nights.
I kept seeing 4:47.
Is that the time he passed away?
In my sleepless nights, I keep noticing when it is 4:47 a.m.

I told my older sister who discovered Angelic Numbers on the Internet. The meaning of 447 is that higher beings are keeping an eye out for me and I am supported and protected. In that moment, my knowing of the angels who protect me was solidified. I had the realization, rock solid in my bones, that God has my back. I couldn't fall because God is here to hold me.

Still.
I feel like I am free falling.
I haven't been able to sleep for a very long time.
I have short spurts of sleep.
In my mind, I ask for my husband to come back to me.
I dream dreams.

I dreamt that my older sister came and told me that my husband was alive.
I couldn't believe it. I ran up the hill to see him.
Love, why did you leave? You are here. I can't believe you are really here.
I have happiness tears in my eyes as I yell at him. How could you do this to us? Disappear like you did. Don't you get how devastating this has been for us?
He just stood there looking at me as I bombarded him with statements and questions.

Then came my realization.
You can't be alive.
I saw you get buried.
How are you here?
He finally spoke.
        My mom noticed that I was still breathing and she had me dug up.

*A sense of immense gratefulness overcomes me for his
mother.*
What happened has happened.
Let's go home now.
*Our kids will be so happy to know you are alive. Let's go
home.*

*I can't come with you. My mother and brother need me. I
must go to them.*

My heart dropped to the ground.
What are you saying? Our kids and I need you.
I was in tears begging him.
Please come to us.
Please come with me.
He told me, You Got This. I must help them.

I woke up heartbroken.
I felt rejected.
I was physically in tears.

I don't Got this.
I don't Got anything.
I will never Get this.

Many months later I dreamt about his brother and mother.
I was yelling at his brother for being deceitful.
How can you live with yourself?
Pretending? When your heart knows the truth.
My kids and I are a unit.
*You can't invite my kids to your daughter's birthday party
and not me.*
You never invited me.
You lie to yourself for denial.
You lie to your parents for self-interest.

*His mother was there and knew I speak the truth. She knew
her favorite son acted in a self-serving manner. She knew
and was sending immense love energy my way.*

———

I woke up from this dream of truths.
I believed my husband is showing me how they needed him
and he must be with them.

With my husband gone, it feels so empty.
I don't like having our bed all to myself now.

I liked it when my girls occupied our bed with me. It made us
all feel just a little safer in the cruel world we existed in.

My younger daughter had nightmares for months. Had I been
able to fall asleep those early months, I may have had
nightmares as well. It was good that I couldn't sleep. I was
there to caress my younger daughter as she talked in her sleep
and screamed in the middle of the night, many a nights. I was
awake to ensure that my older daughter received the hugs
required and the cuddling needed to fall asleep and stay
asleep.

Eventually, I began to sleep for short periods. I felt safe with
my girls around me. My older daughter was always there to
caress me when I would scream in my short spurts of sleep.

*I dreamt I was in San Francisco, driving. I had to go pee and
wanted to rush home. Instead of taking 101 south, the fastest
way home, I knowingly got onto the bridge towards Oakland.
I knew I had to take 101 South. Somehow, I choose to get onto
that bridge. As soon as I was on the bridge with no chance of
return, I started to think to myself 'what is wrong with you?
Why did you go on the bridge when it will take longer to get
home?'*

*Suddenly I thought I want to turn around and go back. Fix
my mistake. I exited to turn around and found myself in a
construction area, unable to get out at all.
What do I do?
How can I get home?*

The next thing I knew, I was at my home with my younger sister there. She was getting ready for a costume party that I was hosting. My younger sister was hassling me to go upstairs and get ready. I saw a costume with a knife going into the person's heart. I told my sister I do not have the time to get ready for this costume party. I needed to go back to San Francisco and get my car that was stuck on the exit on that bridge.

My younger sister then asked: How did you get home if your car is still on the bridge?

I realized I do not have an answer.

I wonder. How did I get home without my car?

I woke up perplexed.

Now my girls are in the process of moving on to their own beds.

I am alone some nights.

In the periods that I fall asleep, I have strange dreams. Maybe even nightmares.

I dreamt I could see my husband asleep in the fetal position on a bed similar to ours. He was asleep in the same position I found him that dreadful morning. I was rushing upstairs to get to him. I couldn't get there because the stairs ended into a ceiling.

I was trying to break the ceiling to get to the room where he lay. This unknown man came to help me break the ceiling. He tried to kiss me. I realized he wasn't interested in helping me break the ceiling. I pushed him off and started yelling. I am trying to get to my husband. Get away from me.

I broke the ceiling with my bare hands.

I got to my husband, who was now standing out of bed.

He was standing there naked.

I ran to hug him.

I said I love you.

He was the same as he was in the coffin.

_____

His temperature was cold.
He had that same smile.
I don't even know who that idiot who kissed me was.
I have been and will always be loyal to you.
He just stood there looking at me unresponsive.
I launched to give him a big loving hug.
He did NOT hug me back.
He could NOT hug me back.

I woke up anxious.
Bewildered.

Seven months after his death is the very next day of this
dream. Pillar Friend picked me up and we went to order my
husband's tombstone. She helped me make major decisions
such as what color stone, what size, pot holder or not, what
shape, picture or no picture, and many a more decisions such
as what to write on the tombstone.

I looked at the display that seemed to have not changed in the
60 years that this small family-owned business of creating
tombstones had been around. The display had a set of stairs
that ended into their ceiling. I gasp.

What did this mean?
Did it mean anything?

I had more and more dreams in the following months.
Then came the most horrible night of my life.

I tossed and turned and could not fall asleep that night.
I heard noises. I got up and walked all over my home. I
checked on my girls.
I went back to my empty bed.
I tossed and turned and still couldn't sleep.
I heard a door bang. My heart dropped. I got up to check my
entire home.
I turned on all the lights downstairs and double-checked all
the windows, doors, and closets.

I walked upstairs and double checked on my girls to make sure they were safe.
I came back to bed once again.
Last I recalled it was 3:18 a.m. I finally must have dozed off.

I dreamt that I am asleep in the same fetal position my husband was asleep.
I recognized this.
I knew I was in our bed. In reality, I was asleep in our own bed in the same fetal position.
Physically, I had been sleeping on the same side my husband used to sleep on.
I was also dreaming it. The setting of the dream was our room in my home.
I was frightened beyond belief.
I sensed this man wearing a black cloak, with a black hood on his head, walking up my home stairs. The same stairs I climbed several times in my non-sleep moments when I heard those sounds.
I left my body and am watching this nightmare from the ceiling of my room.
The man entered my room and I knew he is there behind me.
I could see the whole scene from above.
I could feel it in my being.
The man came to my bed extending his hands as he hovered over me.
I was frightened to death.
Had death come for me?
Strength overcame me.
I physically sat up and turned to look in the face of this creature.
I did not see his face.
The man disappeared in a flash.

I was awake now.
I was sitting in the position of my lucid dream yet I was awake.

My heart beating the fastest it ever had.
I was confused.

Was this a dream or was it real?

The time was 4:11 a.m.

I did not fall asleep again that night. My thoughts took me to awake moments in my life when I looked evil in the face and it disappeared.

The time I was thirteen, walking home from school through a field. I felt someone following me. I stopped, I turned around, and saw a man standing and staring at me. I stared back. I stood still and stared.

He then turned around and walked away. I still stood there staring until he could no longer be seen. Suddenly fright overcame me. I turned around and ran home as fast as I could. I solved my problem by never walking through that field again. I walked along Highway One with fast cars zipping by me. I never took that shortcut through that field, to school, ever again.

My mind took me to my college days when I lived in San Francisco with my older sister. I was at the San Francisco State Library. I pushed the up arrow elevator button. The elevator door opened. I walked in and pushed for the second floor. An Evil man with red hair and freckles wearing blue work overalls was in the elevator. He placed a key in the elevator switch and took us down to the basement.

The elevator door opened in the basement. By the grace of god, I left my body and was watching from the ceiling of the elevator. My body was still. I was staring into this man's eyes, without a blink. There was silence. He stared. I stared. I out stared. He then took his key out of the elevator opening and walked out. I came back into my body. I pushed for the first floor. The elevator door closed and I had a sigh of relief. I had a sigh of fright. The elevator took me back up to the main library floor.

I hurried out and ran to my car to get home. I refused to study at that library ever again. To this day, when alone, I refuse to be in an elevator with a stranger.   My only regret is that I didn't have the understanding back then to report this incident to the university police.

Morning finally arrived.

While helping with deliveries at work, I complained to my work partner how really hard driving was since I had not slept all night due to a bad dream. My work partner asked about it. I described my dream to her.
She was shocked.
I was shocked.

She was finishing my sentences for me. She shared how she had had several of these dreams around 20 years ago. She never had the courage to look the negative creature of a man in the face. She never forgot the dreams and how frightened they made her feel.

How can this be?
How can a person I know have the same exact dream I had?

Exhausted from a full day of physical labor and after a night of mental fright, I contacted my cousin's wife who happens to be Native American. She is my Love Friend, exuding unconditional love like I have never encountered in my life.

Love Friend came to me with her basket of goods. We opened every window and door at my home. We rolled up our sleeves and went to work.

First burning sage and circulating it at every opening.
Then chanting *This is a House of God.*
Only Angels of God are Welcome Here.
Archangel Michael Protects this Home.

Then Love Friend had blessed egg shells and sea shells that were broken into small pieces. We chanted *This is a House of God* as we spread those shells around the inside and outside openings of my home for more protection.

With bare feet touching the ground, we went into the garden to ground ourselves. The feeling of the grass underneath my feet released me. Love Friend dropped down to the grass as if it were snow, making grass angels with her arms and feet. The playfulness was contagious. I lay on the grass next to her. Now I was smiling. I was happy. I was laughing. She cuddled me the same as I had cuddled my older daughter to sleep all those nights. My heart wept from her generosity of soul. I felt safe in the world once again.

Love Friend called her friend's aunt who had been the psychic to Nancy Reagan. Love Friend only said that she is at a friend's home, a friend who was in pain.

Psychic had a vision. The negative force in her home is her in-laws. Anytime a thought of them or any negative thought comes to her mind, tell her to yell *Get Out! This is a House of God!*

I got goosebumps as I heard this.
I had already yelled "Get Out" at the in-laws many a months ago.
How would she know? Love Friend didn't even know.

Psychic went on to say that I had to pick one religion.
One dogma to center myself in.

I am a devout God Lover.
Isn't that religion enough?
I believe in God.
I believe in the Divine.
I believe in the Universal Force.
I believe.

One of the big challenges and questions of my life has been whether by labeling myself and picking a religion I am causing separateness vs. unity. Isn't there a Human Religion?

Anyway, which religion would I pick when I love so many.

I am Muslim.
Do I pray in the Muslim manner every day? No.
Do I empathize with those less fortunate? Yes.

I am Pagan.
Do I treat all matter in this world with respect? No.
Do I praise the change of our seasons and mother earth? Yes.

I am Christian.
Do I go to Bible Study every Sunday? No.
Do I know that Jesus is my savior? Yes.

I am Jewish.
I am Bahai.
I am Budda.
I am Stoic.
I am Taoist.
I am Zoroastrian.
I am Hindi.
I am Wicca.
I am Macumba.
I am Me.
I am God.

The word for God in Persian is KhodA. Khod means Self and A means from. God means "From Self."

I grew up understanding God is within me.
I am of God.
I am God.

The wisdom in identifying with only one religion will be something I have to let simmer for years.

Psychic went on to say that there was a death in my home. She sees a spirit, my husband, in the house protecting my kids and me. My husband is trying to communicate with me and cannot until I unclutter.

Wait a minute. I thought he was already communicating with me.

When my heart ached and I asked my husband to come back to me – The Office Light turned on.
When my heart ached that my son and I were arguing – The TV turned on.
When my heart ached from my husband's sister's treatment of me – The Steam in my shower turned on.
When I wasn't even aware that my heart was aching for my husband – His favorite song started to play on my laptop.

Aren't these communications from my husband?

Later I thought that perhaps his message is for me to unclutter, period.

I used to tell him get rid of your silly old stuff. You know that when you die, I'm going to dump everything. I feel horrible now for having said that to him then. He was a hoarder. I would go around our home uncluttering without him knowing.

With him gone, I can't get myself to throw anything out. A note that has his handwriting is now a treasure. His clothing in the closet gives me solace.

I just can't get myself to unclutter physically.
I sure can't do it mentally.
My brain is so damaged.
I can't keep it straight.
So how in the world does he exactly want me to unclutter???
What a day it has been.
Love Friend left me in a better place when she departed.

———

Shortly afterwards, the phone rang and it was Childhood
Friend wanting to see how I had been.
I told her about my wacky day.
She wasted no time and came right over.
She would spend the night with me.
She wanted to make sure I knew I was not alone.
I never will be alone.
I'm touched beyond life.

Childhood Friend wanted to cover the basics.
> *There is a reason you are not feeling safe at nights.*
> *Do you have an alarm?*
> *Do you turn on your alarm before going to sleep?*

Yes — I did not think we needed an alarm for our home. My
husband insisted we had to install one. The only time the
alarm would go off was for a mistake my kids or I made. Then
I would complain even more to my husband about the silliness
of having an alarm when we didn't even need one.

Now I see how right he was to install one.
Now I'm scared of being home alone.

My alarm had not been working for months.
Childhood Friend rolled up her sleeves and fixed it.
She would tell you she just replaced the batteries.
I will tell you I had not even figured out that it was the
batteries.
I will also tell you that I hadn't done anything for months
about it.
The home alarm went on that night and has been on every
night thereafter.

Then Childhood Friend hit the dreams.
She had me explain my dreams to her.
I took out my laptop to search what my black cloak wearing
man dream meant.
She stopped me.

Don't go to other people's interpretations.
You will find the meaning for you on our own.

We brainstorm.

I started by recalling my recurring childhood nightmares of
being chased down by an animal and not being able to scream.

We end with talking about my real life incidents of falling
while walking up stairs.

Who else in life, while climbing stairs, has broken a toe, badly
hurt a shoulder, bruised and bloodied her body trying to save a
baby in her arm and a toddler holding her hand?
Who else in life, while climbing stairs, has broken her aunt's
wedding china and ended up at the hospital?

The brilliant mind of Childhood Friend found a life pattern.
The pattern? Stairs. Walking up stairs.

It didn't matter what is up those stairs.
I could face it. I could break through it.

I could now go up.

I had been on my knees since this has happened.
I had to get up from the kneeling.
I had to get up myself for the sake of me.
I had to get up and walk.
I had to get up and walk up to God.
I had to get up and walk up to my new life.

I was lifted up by the love surrounding me.

We slumbered together.

I had my first restful night of sleep after nine months.
I only wished it could have been continuous.

———

115

Chapter Nine
Our Relationship

Without a map and unbeknown to me,
I stumbled upon his treasure box of
hidden memoirs.

I had known that I was his one and only
adoration.

Why did he keep memoirs from his
previous affections?

Was he collecting childhood needs not
received?

Was he an emotional hoarder?

Did he ever go back to visit this box?

In our times of hardship did this box give
him an escape?

Was there a fantasy of what might have
been against the reality of the hard work
it took to create what was?

This box broke my heart.
I did not keep such a box.

When asked, my reply is YES.

I am dating.
I am starting to fall in love.

I am dating myself.
I am falling in love with myself.

I miss my husband.
I wish this never had happened.

It did happen.
I am here now.
It is what it is.
I am free now.

Free of his birth family.
Free of his criticisms.
Free of having to satisfy.
Free of having to compromise.

A sense of lightness has taken hold of me.

Bringing these sentiments to the surface is difficult. It has been challenging to come to terms with this feeling of freedom.

When someone we love passes on, we naturally want to idolize and think of all their positive attributes.

My husband was a marvelous citizen of the world.
My husband was a man of service.
He surely had so many positive attributes.
He left a Legacy of better lives in our community with the ripples of giving of his time, money, and self.

My husband was the community member who was on the board of our children's preschool and transformed them from a negative balance to having money in reserves for potential future projects.

My husband was the community member who volunteered in our children's elementary school, bringing his passion for mathematics to children other than his own.

My husband was the community member who gave rides to scholarship kids on our son's competitive soccer team, helping in making it possible for them to participate in club soccer.

One of the greatest legacies he left behind was our smart, athletic, and generous kids.

My husband loved me.
My husband loved his kids.
My husband created a life of goodness for us.

My husband lived life.
Truly Lived life with us.

He would make it happen for us.

Tired of Men's World Cup?
Women's World Cup, here we come.

Tired of California Skiing?
Colorado and Utah, here we come.

My husband was also very difficult to live with.
When we were first married, he would call me into our bathroom to tell me I didn't put the towel back the exact way it needs to be. After 22 years of marriage, he still called me into our bathroom because I didn't close the toothpaste cap all the way.

In my older days, I would just close the toothpaste cap the way he wanted. Smile, kiss him, and tell him I loved him. Show him he was enough.

In my younger days, I would fight.

I'd ask him who decides the exact way the towel needs to be?
You or I?

He would get upset. There is a right way and a wrong way.
I was doing it the wrong way.
He knew the right way.

In our early years of living together, in between the fighting, I
would joke that I'm Sleeping with the Enemy! For people old
enough to recall the movie, my husband was only meticulous.
He was not violent.

At Pillar Friend's wedding, my older sister and I went to the
Ladies Room. I heard a scream from the stall next to me. I
found my older sister in tears.

What happened?

When she was flushing the toilet, the ring her mother-in-law
had gifted her fell in and flushed away.

I told her no worries.
I rolled up my sleeves, got on my knees, and put my hand into
the toilet bowl.

My older sister was shocked. *What are you doing?*

Haven't you seen Sleeping with the Enemy?
Julia Robert's ring came back into the toilet bowl.
I'm sure yours is in there someplace.

And it was.
It was in the pipe behind the actual toilet bowl.
I fished it out.
I found the ring for her.

I found the secret of living with my husband later in our marriage. If we were together for another 24 years it would have been perfect. We truly loved one another. In the midst of our polarization, there remained heavenly physical attraction. There was conviction and loyalty. We realized we were together at the hands of a higher power. We evolved spiritually as a result of our togetherness.

Gone were the days of fighting like crazy, when I wanted him to relax about life. Not everything had to work out the way he wanted it to.

I had now evolved to surrender. That was the secret. Letting go. Surrender.

Was surrender easy to reach? No.
Like everything worth having in life, it required hard work.

The hard work of looking into the mirror to discover what I can do differently.
The hard work of enhancing my physical and spiritual well-being.
The hard work of creating clarity by decluttering my physical world and mind.

I used to think because he was so academically achieved he thought he knew it all.

When I was in my last quarter of college, on a plane ride to the Ford Company in Ohio, the person sitting next to me said you must be at the top of your class if The Ford Company is flying you first class for a job interview.

I truthfully replied that I'm not.

When I got to my interview, I asked why they chose to interview me. The reply was: this is exactly why we are interviewing you. You are curious and ask us an important question. Because you don't have the highest grades, you don't think that you know it all. You are willing to learn. We find that those with just below high grades are more open to learn and work in teams.

So there. I had below high grades and could work in teams. My husband was the academic genius. But man, was it ever hard to for my husband to team up with me. I learned to live with that.

My husband was conscientious. He cared about rules. He took his duties seriously. He was a workaholic. He was meticulous and inflexible. And did he ever hate mistakes. He hated making it and couldn't bear it when I made any mistakes.

I would remind him mistakes are learning. We have to keep making them so we can keep improving.

If I put too much pepper in our food, he would be upset beyond belief. I would tell him, if I killed someone, you would be more understanding than the silliness of putting more pepper in our food. I am a creative cook. I look at what we have and put together dishes without recipes. He had always hoped I could follow recipes to the 'T'.

I would laugh to lighten up the mood. He would be upset at my laughing, claiming I was making light of a serious situation.

He demanded perfection from himself and from me. This caused a lot of pressure and stress in our lives. It was a matter of life and death to him that we were immaculate with our word. We looked flawless, we were flawless, and we lived flawless.

I would remind him how lucky he was. After all, I was already so close to flawless!! I just need to practice giving loving words to myself.

How did I survive those unbearable years? When we had young children, he worked long hours and hardly came home yet expected that I do it all without help. I had to work, take care of our son, and take the garbage out. I downsized. No more work. No more taking the garbage out. I couldn't do it all anymore.

How did I endure when he gave more priority to soccer than being there for me?

I recall the night I needed milk for our son, I called and begged him to come home where he was needed. I needed him to bring milk and relieve me of my exhaustion. He said No he is busy. I yelled at him. What kind of a husband and father are you? He then sent his brother to bring me milk and went off to his soccer practice straight from work.

I recall the day a pregnant me put our son in a stroller and decided to walk to the school where my husband's team was playing soccer. I wanted to surprise him and watch his game. After the game was over, he came over surprised and happy to see us.

Yet, my husband informed me that he is going to lunch to celebrate with his teammates. I told him I'm too tired to walk back home. Please give us a ride home. His solution to the "problem" was handing me his car keys. He then caught a ride to lunch with his friend.

I realized that there is no car seat in his car. How will I transport my toddler? I picked up the stroller to place in the backseat with my toddler in it. I tried to make it as snug as possible for the drive.

A complete stranger stopped to check in on me, asking me if I was okay and how he could help. Tears overcame me. I was not okay. Why didn't my husband check on me? Why didn't my husband ask me if I needed any help?

I made it home. I came inside with my son and luckily forgot to lock the front door.

Stressed, Drained, and in massive Pain, I started bleeding heavily. I made it to the bathroom. I saw the fetus that was my unborn child in the toilet. After the heavy bleeding stopped, I came out to find my toddler playing in the living room. I must have fainted there next to him.

My younger sister and her husband were in the neighborhood and had decided to stop by, only as angels would. The front door was unlocked, as God would have it. They found my son and me in the state of disarray. They helped with my son. They helped me restore myself. My younger sister's husband was upset. This is not right, he kept repeating. My younger sister made me go in to see a gynecologist. It was at this point that I was encouraged by my family to get a nanny to help me. No more doing it all on my own. My parents took a stance and made this very clear.

The mourning of the loss of my unborn Dragon Child, I was able to process by writing, as I now process the loss of my beloved. I wrote a cruel letter to my husband to release my feelings. At the time, I didn't have the courage to give that letter to him.

After my husband's passing, when clearing through his papers, I discovered he had saved that venting letter I had written. I had no idea. He never mentioned knowing about the letter to me. Tears overcame me as I read the letter I had written so many years ago. How I blamed him for the loss of my unborn Dragon Child. How I had wanted him to step up and be a real man. Be a man who protects and stands up for his wife. Be a man who is there for his child. Be a man who takes out the garbage and comes home for dinner.

That letter must have been his reminder in life to be there for us.

Once when clearing out my parents' papers, I found a letter addressed to my parents from the early nineteen sixties. It was from Mary, an American woman living in Ahvaz, Iran. She was being thankful to my parents for their support, love, and understanding. My mother had kept the letter as a reminder that she should have done more. Mary later committed suicide and left behind two young children. She could no longer endure the pressures placed on her by her husband, her husband's family, and the Iranian society. She felt trapped and saw no other escape.

I am fortunate to have survived those early years. I look back now and realize I was able to endure for so long because I was blind.

I was blind because of physical attraction.
I was blind because of moral obligation.
I was blind because of love shared.

I was also just in survival mode.

I did not understand my hardships.
Childhood Friend understood my hardships.
I didn't know it to tell.
Childhood Friend knew it to act.

Now looking back, I see how Childhood Friend was there like a rock, reminding me who I have always been and who I am.

Reinforcing me, the woman of strength.
Reinforcing me, the woman of courage.

The one who is a survivor of sexual abuse.
The one who continually advances herself.
The one who has clarity to see and courage to say.
The one who became an engineer at the young age of 21.
The one who made money at a young age to buy a house.
The one who lives by her own standards, not societal rules.
The one who knows that right is right, even if only one person does it.
The one who knows that wrong is wrong, even if every person does it.

Childhood Friend was there to lift sinking me out of the water, time and time again, making sure I do not drown in the criticisms of life and my husband. She recognized her father in my husband. She had known it to handle it.

My cousin in Oregon had stage four colon cancer. He had told me about all the symptoms that he had ignored, such as nausea. Finally, when he went in to see the doctor, it was too late. As he shared his experience with me, I saw myself in his words.

Oh my God. I have cancer too. I went to visit the doctor, convinced I had a serious illness. I was asked if I had done a pregnancy test. I said no. I already have two children. I'm not pregnant. At some subconscious level, I preferred to die instead of having another child. Please check my vitals and run other tests. I'm sure it must be cancer.

The doctor came back to give me the great news. *You are pregnant. Congratulations.*

I was shocked.

I started to bawl.

I'm pregnant?

I can't handle two children.

I can't handle my life.

How will I handle a third child?

Really I just can't keep my head above water.

Why am I pregnant?

The doctor gently asked me to go home to my husband and discuss my concerns.

I went to a home where my husband was always at work. One of our greatest disagreements was that I wanted to remodel our home and felt I needed a different space. He felt like we were fine. I would remind him that he is never home. I am NOT fine. By the way, how is your affair with work coming along?

We were finally able to discuss our third child situation at home. He felt that two children were more than enough for our family. Sure, we can have three children, just not now. Maybe we can have another child sometime in the future.

I had calmed down and felt we should welcome a child now that there is a knock at our door. What does a time in the future even mean?

He went into a mathematical calculation for me. *I only help you now 20% of the time with two children. If you wish to keep this third child, you are on your own. I will still be helping the same amount of time. However, the percentage will decrease because the workload will increase, blah blah* blah.

I got my voice and all the voices of downtrodden women in me.

I had believed in you.

I had believed in us.

I am keeping my child.

I would never return a gift from God.
I will handle life on my own.
Don't give yourself so much credit. Helping 20% of the time?
You are never around.
You help 0% of the time.

I don't need you.
I had hoped for a real husband.
I had hoped for a real family.
I will be just fine on my own.
Thank-You.
Good-Bye.

He did not accept my departure.

I had begged him to see a marriage counselor throughout the
early years of our marriage but to no avail. He approached me
and suggested we talk to someone and resolve our child
conflict.

And so we did.
And so he discovered the future is now.
And so I prevailed.
And so our younger daughter was born in peace.

I again felt the power of God in my heart the first time I held
our younger daughter.

I had received what I had dreamt about.
I had received the gift of a sister for my daughter.

I had received more than I could have dreamt about.
I had received the gift of a husband for me.
I had received the gift of a father for my children.

After our third child was born, my husband had a turning
point in life.

He became the man I had believed in.
He became the man I had thought in my mind I married.
He became the man who helped out 80% of the time.

I had given up the dream of one day remodeling our home. I came to a place of surrender on the issue and comprehended his long held belief that if we build a home together, we might get a divorce. I loved him and understood he didn't want to risk our marriage.

The change in him was so stark. He stepped up unexpectedly and made the biggest sacrifice of his life—building a home of dreams for his family. At the start of our home project, he gave me a necklace as a gift. The necklace reads "Believe, Dreams come true."

I love being home. Every moment in every wall, door, and window, I feel the testament of his love. I see it in the two H's on our Happy Home door. I see it in our heart-shaped pool. I see it in the design of our mudroom that holds soccer gear.

I love my necklace on my neck and never want to take it off.
I believed in him to be the husband I required.
He became.

Didn't I get what I had come to get.
Why am I still here?

The shift was so immediate that at times I pinched myself and wasn't sure I knew the person I was living with. As good as life was, there was still compromise and keeping each other satisfied.

I had a creative epiphany and produced a design that included my blessings, our three children, and a representation of the prosperous life we were living.   I wanted to solidify this design as a small tattoo on my leg. He adamantly was against tattoos. It put him over the edge. He told me he would leave me if I got one. I never got that tattoo. My life was too good to rock my relationship for a tattoo.

He helped make our kids lunches.
He helped with rides to their activities.
He spent quality family time.
He made sure our days were filled with laughter and love.

I made sure he knew how grateful I was.
I made sure God knew how grateful I was.

Before when things were going good, I would be afraid of losing the goodness.
I was so afraid that I would jinx goodness that I downplayed any blessings.
I had evolved to let go of that fear.
I had evolved to replace fear with gratefulness.

How does our world work?
How can goodness be taken away from me?
I was immensely grateful.
I was cognizant and appreciated every moment.

I often wondered and questioned what made him be remorseful and have a shift in behavior? What made the drastic shift in my husband? He would reply, he had always been this wonderful I just never took notice.

Maybe this was the time period he found my cruel letter.
Maybe this was the time period God found his heart.

He already had a huge heart full of love.
He now became a man I could rely on.

He still reverted to a wounded child when his parents were visiting from Iran.

Everything had to be perfect for them.
He would be so tense prior and during the visits.

It took me a long time to figure it out. When his parents were visiting he would transform into a small child, seeking acceptance and love. When I finally understood the extent of his wounded being, I stopped nagging at him to relax and my heart moved for him.

I'm most grateful for this discovery. It taught us to ensure that our children knew they were loved and accepted by us. Unconditional love. Knowing they are enough.

I would keep our calendar free of any commitments for the duration of his parents' visits. For that time we had no friends, no life. We waited for the chance to visit with them. Did they visit? Not much. It was mostly begging on my husband's part to be able to see them. Phone calls my husband would make wanting to make plans to see his parents only to be told *let's wait and see what happens.*

In the week that my husband passed, he had his last phone call with his mother in Iran. He extraordinarily spoke for a very long time.

Did he know what was ahead? Did his soul realize he would be transformed into a different realm in a short period of time?

Based on past experience, I figured he was telling her I'm here.
See me.
Hear me.
Love me.
My heart went out to him that one last time when he was talking with her.

I kissed him.

I reinforced that I see you.
I reinforced that I love you.

He was always working so hard to make that connection.
His mother must have finally given him what he required.
Being Enough. Belonging. Loved.

My husband must have gotten what he had come to get.
Why else would he leave?

My husband's mother played a dirty game of comparison in
the earlier years of my marriage. I witnessed the make-believe
world where my husband's younger brother was somehow
superior. Why my husband's mother had to create
comparison in her mind baffled me for years. How for years
she called me by her Favorite Daughter-in-law's name. How
my husband's brother's name was on her lips when she spoke
with my husband.

How many times I had to endure illogical comments.
The summer I spent in Iran, my husband's mother told me
how her younger son is so successful, he makes more money,
has more real estate, and drives a BMW. This success is
because of his wife. And with condemnation she stated, *I don't
know why your husband is not successful. Is it because of
you?*

I know she grew more distaste for me when I informed her
that my husband is in fact monetarily very successful. I hardly
doubt his brother's income matches. We have kids and
manage our money differently than they do. Labels on cars are
not important to me. We built our own life and bought our
own homes, cars and more. Can your younger son truly say
the same?

My husband's mother would then imply that I'm jealous of her
trust fund son and Favorite Daughter-in-law.

I would go on to explain, Lady, our riches you have no clue about. Our riches and success are in our life lived, our children's being, and our love spent. I kept telling her about our riches. I kept telling her about our children.

My husband's mother did it again in the week of my husband's passing. Sitting in my older sister's family room and telling me that my husband didn't make enough money. I asked her, what would I have done with more money? We had a rich life. Do you realize he is gone? He will not be coming back? Do you realize more money is not important? We already lived privileged lives. Will you ever say that he was enough for you? Now that he is gone, will you please admit he was enough?

Words spoken.
Words understood.
Meanings not comprehended.

What a toll this mindset put on my husband.
What a toll this mindset put on my husband's brother.

He has a good heart, my husband's brother.
Had he left Iran by the age of 15 to be free of cultural and parental influence and grow into his own person in the United States, he would have been a courageously authentic version of the person he is today. He did not. He was in Iran until his mid-twenties. He finished university there and served in the military by doing office work. He was influenced by the post-revolution culture. He came into being under the influence of his parents and now wife. He became indecisive and a follower. One thing I hated to witness is how his wife and their friends dump on him. Once he moved to the United States, he began to wrestle in his mind with his past beliefs as he grew in the capacity to expand his being. I can see it as clear as day. My husband's brother has a quest to learn to become a better version of himself.

Still, the toll of being a "favorite" brings about unconscious feelings.

In my family, the first grandchild and my niece, gave the name called by all grandchildren to my parents. In most loving families, I know this is the norm. The first grandchild sets precedence. Using the same name for grandparents brings unity to a family. Our son, being the first grandchild in my husband's family, gave the names to his paternal grandparents.

My husband's brother made sure my son's given names not be used and made his own names that he worked so hard to teach his child to repeat after him. This act of separatism from his own brother and nephew was heartbreaking for my husband.

What a relief it must have been for him when his brother/my husband passed. No more carrying the heaviness of being a "favorite" in your mother's eyes.

Now my husband is no more.
Now the favoritism is no more.
Now my husband's brother can breathe.
Now my husband's mother can mourn my riches lost.

Do we naturally gravitate to one child over another?
As a mother I can say, to various degrees yes.

Do we have the awareness to make each child feel enough?
Do we have the awareness to make each child feel loved?
As mothers, we had better.
When we don't, we give to society childlike adults in need of acceptance.

Not everything in life is your mother's fault.
Maybe it is your authoritative grandfather's fault.
Life is complicated.

Part of it is personality.
Part of it is needs met.

As mothers, we have so much influence.

135

We have a duty to ensure our children know, feel, and sense they are enough.

Once children know they are enough,
I think this need to be perfect will be gone.
This need to be right can disappear.
This need to control will be no more.

As adults who didn't have perfect mothers, we must allow ourselves to feel enough. We must be kind, gentle, and loving to ourselves.

Do I miss my husband?
Of course I do.
Every Day.

All the days I am responsible for thinking through and making decisions. Even though I shouldn't make the major ones, I'm told, for at least the first year.

Do we rent our home and move in with my older sister?
My kids' lives have already turned upside down and adding a move may not be a healthy choice for them. Communal living may be the only healthy choice for me.

Do I tell my older daughter's friend's mother that my husband passed?
I like to share that I have lost my husband. If I say it, maybe I can start to believe it. My older daughter seeks normality. She hasn't shared her personal loss with her friends at school because that is the one place life can continue as was.

Do we get a dog for my younger daughter who wants one?
A dog is what she needs for her mental well-being but how will I handle the extra responsibility of caring for a dog? I miss my husband.
I do.
Every Day.

The day I got a flat tire in the morning and then got a call from
school because my older daughter had a massive headache and
blurry vision. I missed him. I cried. He would have taken
care of one while I took care of the other. I don't have time to
breathe because I have to take care of both.

I miss him.

The day I have to take care of laundry and computer problems.
The day I have to take care of carpool and health insurance
non-payments.
The day I have to take care of dinner and fix the tripping water
pump.
The day I have to take care of this and that and everything.
The day I want to have an adult conversation.
The day I want to be held.

I miss him every single day.

I'm overwhelmed.
I can't breathe.
I can't keep up with life.
I can't keep up with me.

I am learning.
I am learning to be with myself.
I am learning to love myself.
I am learning to be gentle and kind to myself.

I am learning to adjust to my newfound freedom.

I have Freedom to make decisions.
I have Freedom to make responsibilities.
I have Freedom to make hope.
I have Freedom to make peace.
I have Freedom to make freedom.

Chapter Ten
Bullying

Are the two faces of you really just one?

During the Summer I spent in Iran with my children of ages 2, 4½, and 7, one day our younger daughter was upset as a normal two-year-old should be from time to time. She was having a tantrum. I was doing my best to hold her and tell her that I loved her. My husband's mother, clearly annoyed by the noise, came over to say that she does not like bad children who cry. While I understood that this statement was a circumstance of her generation and environment, it nonetheless startled me. I whispered in our younger daughter's ear that good children cry all the time. You are precious and loved.

I myself have had bad behavior. It doesn't mean I am a bad person.

Words are important. I made an effort to reinforce that our children are good, even though they may have bad behavior at times. Emphasis was always placed on changing the bad behavior. Their core I know to be love.

In our nation we use the word "Bully" to describe people who are being mean or terrorizing others.

"The Bully" is a human being who has displayed the bad behavior of intentionally harming physically or emotionally over time to intimidate and maintain power. This behavior is unacceptable. This should not mean that the person is unacceptable. The person is redeemable.

Bullying is a sophisticated, calculated, and manipulative act to gain control. It requires some level of maturity. Small children testing their limits are not bullying.

Bullying is acts of meanness repeated towards the same person. A one-time act of meanness is just meanness.

Bullying is typically done in isolation without witnesses the recipient can depend on.

Bullying also happens amongst adults. I love that as a nation we focus on our future, the adolescents, and bringing awareness and solutions to this age group for a better future.

Bullying occurs online, among siblings, families, friends, workplace, schools, communities, and organizations.

The number one excuse for the bad behavior of bullying is "we are different." This is the basis of all such behavior—seeing oneself different from or superior to.

This is why hate begins.
This is why war begins.
This is what death ends.

Having volunteered for well over a decade in our kids' school, I was well versed in Conflict Resolution vs. Bullying Boundaries. I made the association that conflict existed for adults. Mature adults come together and share their view of an issue in order to achieve a win-win solution. I had been blind to the adult world of bullying.

In all these years, I had never associated my own interactions with my husband's family with bullying. It took a professional counselor to point out the textbook bullying interactions my husband's family displayed towards me. I had been victim to a classic case of "Family Bullying", in-law bullying, for so long and I had not even realized it.

I knew I felt bad as a result of interacting with them. I knew they saw me as an outsider and not as their family member. I heard the mean words and the derogatory comments. My heart knew it to be wrong. My mind hadn't figured it out.

I realize now that this behavior was to build a strong bond within my husband's family Herd. Having the hatred of me in common gave their togetherness purpose.

Once I made the realization that I had been a target for my husband's family, it all made sense. Over two decades of interactions made sense. All the events after his passing made sense.

I now felt a sense of relief.
I felt lighter.
I could understand.
I now knew what I was dealing with.
I now had the resolution to get the right tools to handle it.

It had been a challenge from day one. The first day I met my future husband's parents, I was so excited. They were flying into San Francisco International Airport, SFO. I brought flowers and the two of us waited to greet them with the biggest smiles on our faces.

What would I say to his parents?
I'm so grateful that you have brought the man that I love into the world?
I am so grateful that you have raised my soul mate?
Thank you for taking him to soccer games as a child?

My heart was beating fast to meet his parents for the first time after we had been together for over a year. I said hello and offered the flowers to my future mother-in-law. She looked me in the eye, didn't say a word, didn't take the flowers, and walked away. I was stunned. My future father-in-law tried to compensate for this behavior. He said hello and maintained a minimal conversation with me.

My future mother-in-law had one of two choices to make:
Accept with Love.
Reject with Hate.

My future mother-in-law Accepted me with Hate. Rejected me with Love.

Years later, after we had been married with children, I experienced a Deja Vu. My husband's mother at SFO not replying to my welcome hello. I thought maybe she didn't realize I said hello. I went up to her face to ask her how her long trip had been. I got the dirty look and off she walked.

On this trip, she made sure I understood that she was not going to bring the "garbage" Samovar her mother had gifted me. I couldn't figure it out. Was she upset that her mother had gifted me a family heirloom?

On this same trip, she made sure I understood that she brought the family silver for clever Favorite Daughter-in-law. My husband's mother was proud of how Favorite Daughter-in-law had managed to get all her family silver for herself.

My husband's mother was correct about me not paying attention to material objects. I can see how I frustrated her. Every Persian bride gets the gift of Mirror and Candlesticks to be used at her wedding ceremony and every winter solstice and spring equinox thereafter.

When we were first married, our living space was so minimal that I had no room to display all the lovely gifts bestowed upon us. My mom had the great idea of packing my things up and placing them in a storage unit. So I did. My dad owns a storage facility. I asked my dad for a small unit just for myself. He insisted that the small ones were all rented and I could have a larger unit all to myself.

Years later, in an effort to find my wedding silver candlesticks, I went to my storage unit to bring back my stuff. I found the lock on my unit had been changed. I was able to get the new key and discovered that the storage was full of other people's stuff as well. My dad had offered a non-profit organization to store their auction objects in my storage unit. I took all my stuff out in search of my wedding candlesticks and could not find them.

I was fuming at my dad.
How could you allow others to store in my unit without asking
me?

I was fuming at my mom.
How could you suggest that I take my stuff to a storage that is
unpredictable?

I was fuming at myself.
How could I not know what happened to my wedding
candlesticks for so many years?

I was fuming at my husband.
If your mother asks me where those candlesticks are one more
time, I will explode.

I came to believe that the non-profit organization sold my
wedding candlesticks at their auction. I finally made peace
that the money went to help needy children. I accepted what
was.

Once I made peace, my older sister's words sunk in. It is okay
to ask your husband's mother to bring you another candlestick
set from Iran. My older sister's glass Mirror and Candlesticks
came from the island of Murano in Italy. In the first year she
was married, one of the candlesticks broke. Her mother-in-
law was moody too. Nice one minute, mean the next. My
older sister told her mother-in-law about her broken
candlestick. Her mother in-law flew to Italy and went back to
Murano. She walked with a picture of the candlesticks to every
store for a week. Finally, a merchant took pity on her. She
was invited to the merchant's basement to look through what
was stored down there on her own accord. She found the
matching candlestick for her son and my older sister to bring
back to the United States.

My plight was much simpler. My candlestick picture could be given to a silver maker in Iran to be custom made. No flying to a foreign country for my husband's mother or walking around with a picture for a week.

My older sister and her husband had come over to our home one evening and my husband's mother happened to call. She was coming to the United States and lovingly she was calling to see if we needed anything. So I had my husband, my older sister, and her husband in front of me encouraging and rooting for me to ask.

I did. I asked. I asked for a pair of candlesticks from Iran. My husband's mother got confused. Then I put it into blunt words for her. I have lost my wedding candlesticks. I was hoping you would give the picture to a silver maker in Iran who can custom make my wedding candlesticks for me.

Oh my God.
My jaw dropped at the onset of her reaction.

You are a *deserveless* (Biliaghat) human being.
You are the reason my son is living below his worth.
You are not even the little finger of your husband's sister and Favorite Daughter-in-law.

I was shocked. I had figured she didn't like me. I just hadn't realized the extent of it until that moment. I was embarrassed that my older sister, her husband, and my husband were witnessing this as a group.

After she got done belittling my being.

Because Favorite Daughter-in-law has so much silver and I can't even keep my wedding silver.
Because my husband's sister drives a luxury car and I don't.
Because I don't push my husband to make more money and I should.

I gave her my two cents.

I am more concerned about the well-being of my family rather than silver.
I am an American and buy cars that support work in the United States.
I am not attached to money. I am proud to be attached to love.

Your son lives his worth. We live a life of privilege. What would we do with more money that we don't do now? You see your daughter and Favorite Daughter-in-law as superior to me. I see them having inauthentic lives and lost souls.

Lady, my riches you will never be able to comprehend. My riches are in a husband who adores, appreciates, and acknowledges me. My riches are in my healthy and happy children. My riches are in my life of love spent and peace received.

My older sister apologized to me. She finally realized why I was afraid to mention anything about this to my husband's mother. It wasn't me as my older sister had thought. It was my husband's mother.

My husband realized how serious the situation with his mother was.

In that interaction, I made a decision. I will not initiate any contact with my husband's mother again. The few times my husband asked me to call his mother, I did for him. I had used to call her on my own to tell her about her grandchildren. I had used to call her so she could hear something cute from her grandchildren on the phone. I stopped. I stopped cold turkey.

Her ungratefulness.
Her belief that she, her daughter, and Favorite Daughter-in-law are better than.
Her thinking she knows better than.
It killed any hope for a potential loving relationship.

Years later, after the rebuilding of our home, I was opening boxes and found my wedding candlesticks. I couldn't believe it because mysteriously it was in a box that didn't make sense timeline wise in my life. I couldn't believe that after 20 years those candlesticks came back to us. Destiny.

After my husband shared the news of our finding to his mother, she gifted us another set of silver candlesticks with a matching mirror! Why? Why after a decade of her crude comments to me would she bring such a gift? This is a gift meant for new brides. Is she saying she wants to turn back the clock and start fresh with us? Or was she reminded of what she had said to me? Was it guilt? Was it a way to say she was sorry for her truth? Although the gift wasn't too little, wasn't the sentiment far too late?

I could not guess her intent.
She did not share her intent.
The damage was done with no sign of remorse for over a decade.
The gift meant nothing to me.

Once any hope for a potential loving relationship is killed, it is killed. There is hard work to be done in resurrecting. Shared intent is a big first step. Niceness and living with love every day for as long as it would take to mend a relationship is the answer. Not an extravagant gift having no significance.

If I weren't so naïve and blind in my younger years, I should have seen the extent of her hatred for me from the beginning. From the outset, my husband's parents did not approve of our union. I realized the pressure this put on my future husband. Sting's lyrics *If you love somebody, set them free* played through my mind. I decided I would set him free. I truly felt that if his family did not approve of our marriage, it doesn't make sense for us to be together. I was good with my decision. Sure, I would have loved to spend the rest of my life with him. I also knew if I didn't spend the rest of my life with him, I would have been just fine.

Prior to meeting my husband in my early twenties, there was a lovely family who had been friends with my mom's family for many a years. This couple had been to my parents' wedding. My maternal grandparents had attended their wedding. Their youngest son, six years my senior was a good looking, tall, and a smart young man who founded a software company back in the late 1980's. His father would write me poetry. His mother showered me with love. I like to live with the flow, I was willing to marry him and into his family of love who seemed to appreciate me before I even appreciated me.

I started to sense this guy is not telling me the truth. I found out he was double timing me. He told me he was planning to get married with me and only having a good time with his administrative assistant. This was wrong on so many levels, which made it easy for me to walk away. My parents always supported me in such decisions. Others made comments like, "What will people think?" "Don't you want to be financially comfortable for the rest of your life?" My parents understood me. I hardly care what people think. I'm not attached to money that comes and goes when it pleases.

Well, my future husband didn't take my walking away from him so lightly. I'm not sure what went down with his parents and him. He came back to formally declare he was not going to live without me and gave me a book: Everything men know about women. The entire book was blank.

My future husband and his parents later came to formally ask for my hand from my parents, as is tradition in many cultures. His mother, with her superior attitude, mentioned to my mom that she had not sent her son to the United States to marry just "any" girl. My mom assured her that her daughter is not just "any" girl. My dad, taken aback by this comment, talked about the importance of love and choosing one's own mate in life as he had decades before with my mom.

The meanness continued beyond my husband's lifetime. Alongside the mean comments was what I presumed to be guilt that precipitated astounding gifts of jewelry.

Prior to going back to Iran, my husband's mother gave me the most beautiful high grade South American emerald and diamond ring. The first of many jewels that I treasure now to be passed down in the future to my daughters, a future daughter-in-law, and grandchildren.

The next time my husband's parents came to the United States was for our wedding. I don't recall seeing my husband's mother much anywhere during our reception and just barely at the wedding ceremony. In later years, my husband's mother shared that an old friend was confiding in her and kept her in the bathroom for hours during our wedding. I always felt it was her own loss if she didn't care enough to be fully present.

What is it about the mother-in-law and daughter-in-law relationship?
Is no one in the world good enough for her son?
Is it the new generation that is threatening?
The loss of youth realized?

Is it those mother- in-laws who never experience true love and are now jealous of their son's affection and love for another?

I was confused.
Her son had been her son for a short 15 years.
He would have been recruited for the Iran-Iraq war.
He had to leave Iran overnight.
He went to Austria.
He lived with an Austrian family.
He went to high school in Austria.

My husband's parents were unsuccessfully trying so hard to get him the proper visas to go to England where he could have been with his Uncle's family. On a destiny shaping day a friend living in the United States asked, *why England*? I will sponsor your son to come to the best country in the world, the United States of America.

And so he did. He did the work of angels.

My husband ended up in Utah when he was 16.
He lived in the university dormitory while finishing high school. He got a scholarship and attended University of Utah studying Electrical Engineering. He was so smart he finished in 3 years and ended up at Stanford University in California for his graduate school.

He was really smart.
He was really alone.

In the early months after we had met, when I was on business trips and in calling home, I would find my future husband hanging out with my family having dinner and playing cards. I would be dumbfounded. What if we break up? He was not supposed to be all chummy with my family.

The next time his mother got to be in his life, he was already in mine. He was already in my birth family's life.

Is that what made her dislike me?

Or was it that her son had chosen to love me?
Was it that we came from different cultures?
Was it different belief systems?
Was it different values?
We were different.
Shouldn't differences and diversity be celebrated?

We were the same.
Really weren't we the same?

I think if a person loves my child.
Wants to spend the rest of their lives with my child.
Wants to raise a family with my child.
Wants to build a life with my child.

I would get to know them.
I would find commonalities with them.
I would find their strengths to celebrate.
I would love them.
I would be grateful.
I would love them more.

I think. I have yet to experience. My husband's mother did
this. She loved her other daughter- in-law. Then loved her
more. Made a point of it to me. Made a point of it to my
family.

The time my husband's mother was in Berlin and my Aunts
took her out to dinner. My Aunts were in disbelief. The
message back to me was your mother-in-law talked about how
wonderful her other daughter-in-law was the entire night. My
Aunts joked with me and said dinner was a boxing match. She
threw a punch and then we threw two punches of highlighting
your goodness!!

The time my husband's mother visited my home asking to see the decorative object that Favorite Daughter-in-law gifted me. I told her I had not received such a gift, so I didn't have it to show. She indicated that I was lying. *Favorite Daughter-in-law bought this for you when I was with her.* I said maybe she changed her mind and kept it. I do that sometimes, buy something for someone and then think I really like it myself. Truly, this is okay to do. I don't need any more objects in my life. My husband's mother maintained that I was lying to her.

The time I made general comments about the wrongs of breastfeeding while intoxicated especially when the newborn is taking medication. My husband's mother making it clear that Favorite Daughter-in-law is smart, capable, and doesn't need advice from lowly jealous me. My husband made it clear to me, in private, that even if his brother and Favorite Daughter-in-law are killing their own child, we are not to interfere.

The time in Mexico when Favorite Daughter-in-law wobbly walked towards us and then fainted in the middle of the afternoon. My young kids were surprised and concerned asking what had happened. I was working in my mind on a sympathetic reply along the lines of how we must live our heart's calling so that we don't have to numb ourselves with drugs. My husband's mother beat me to the punch, explaining that Favorite Daughter-in-law is full of life and happiness. *How we need to learn from her to live our life to its fullness.*

Did she just encourage my kids to use drugs?

My husband's mother, she was a not a hard one to figure out. Her favorite son was my husband's brother and his wife was her favorite daughter-in-law. She made sure we knew of this fact.

My husband knew this fact.
This broke my heart.

I could care less about his mother and her silly favorite games she played. What concerned me more was this thought: does she not like me because she can't stand her own son?

I cared for and loved my husband. He, I would go to bat for.

Before we had children and we were both working, we sent some money to Iran to buy the now famous apartment in a high rise that was being built in Tehran. The worst investment ever. After we made the purchase, his parents gifted my husband's brother in the same building the same type apartment. I was stunned. Who does that?

I went to bat for my husband. On one of their trips to the United States, I gave them a piece of my mind. Let's say I had two children and one worked hard to buy his own bike, by buying the same exact bike for the second child I have devalued the hard work of the first child. I can buy a car for the second child, just not the same exact bike.

Man Oh Man. This statement was one my husband's mother would never understand nor forget. Maybe she never forgot it because she still needs to fully understand it.

My husband's mother came to the following conclusion:

You are jealous.
You are materialistic.
You want us to buy you real estate.
You are after our money.

All ridiculously untrue. Anyone who knows me, including myself, can confirm. In her mind, this was her truth. And thus became the truth in the minds of her Herd.

Did my husband die of a broken heart?

My husband's mother and her daughter stopped by our home at the insistence of my husband during one of his parents' visits to the United States. As they usually did when they came to our home, they just wanted to get out and leave as soon as possible. Despite my offering tea and working hard to start a pleasant conversation, she was not budging. Then came the hit. *We are running late. Your father and I have a family portrait planned with your sister, brother, and his wife. We need time to get ready.*

My jaw dropped.
They left.

My husband was perplexed. Are we not family?
I told him our kids and I are not family.
You are.
Of course you are.

I knew he was not.
Of course he was not.

What broke my heart was when I would walk into a room and their conversations would stop as a result or worse being in a room when whispers or looks would take place without regard to my presence.

What broke my husband's heart the most was going to restaurants with his Herdish Family. We would be on time even when we had small kids. My husband's brother and his wife would show up late. When they showed up, without fail, they would make us get up and move seats so they could sit next to the parents.

This was the most repulsive act of all. I would catch my husband's look. He never said anything, always just observing and knowing.

The last time we experienced this was in London for his parents' anniversary dinner. I told my husband in advance, let's just sit at the end of the table. He said no, *in the middle. I want to see if they'll move us.*

I think he knew he didn't have much longer to live at some subconscious level. I think he had hoped they wouldn't suggest we move. I think he had hoped they would embrace him and his wife of over two decades. He was looking for that confirmation from them. He was always looking. They just weren't capable of giving. We were asked to move to the end of the table. My heart broke for him.

That was the last trip I would take with his family. His parents were going to Paris for their wedding anniversary. His parents decided to go to England to close some loose ends with my husband's uncle's family. I had not wanted to go. My husband insisted that he wanted me to be there with him. I hated the uncomfortable feeling around his family and just wanted to live in peace. It was important to him, so for the love of my husband, we left our kids behind and I went.

As soon as my husband's sister found out I was going, it turned into a big ordeal. My husband's brother and his wife had to be there too, if I'm going to be there. This has been the story of our lives with them. If I'm doing something, God forbid they fall behind. If I'm going to be someplace, God forbid they are not there too.

We went to Paris. My husband and I had alone time together, which I will always treasure. In addition to our alone time was the uncomfortable time, even after two decades of being with his family.

The women of the family looking at the emblem on my purse, dying to figure out what brand it is. The Shallowness of their being had always been a sour point with me. To entertain myself at times, I played the game of checking out their purses making sure they knew I was doing it. Or was I trying to show them the tackiness of that act?

During the trip to Paris and London, as with other trips, I was cordial to them. They were my husband's family. I tried my best to get the confirmation from them that he was seeking. I laughed with them. I conversed with them. I was just always uncomfortable with them.

I had bought my husband's parents an anniversary present. And took the time to create a speech focusing on their positive attributes and being grateful for their being. My anniversary present was, purposefully, a picture framed of our three kids. Pushing my kids on them. Love them, here they are.

When my son was born, I thought the tide had changed. My husband's mother was at the hospital and spent the night with me. She was so happy and so kind to me during this time. She cared so much by getting up in the middle of the night to help.

After a couple of weeks of being home, I had wanted to go to a Toastmasters meeting one afternoon. I hadn't been to a meeting for months and prior to giving birth had attended every week. I thought that since my in laws are only in the United States for a short time longer, they'd want to spend time with our son before going back. My husband's mother boldly stated that she had not come to the United States to be my babysitter. I tried to explain that it is a short meeting, and the only reason I asked was because I thought she'd want to spend time with her grandchild before going back to Iran. Really, I wasn't asking her to be my babysitter while I was off at work.

I took my son to go to my mom's who was more than happy at the chance to spend the time with her new grandson. At this point my husband's father came to my car and asked me for the privilege of spending time with their grandson.

Years later, on one of their trips to the United States, she did babysit for her favorite son and daughter-in-law when they went to a party in San Francisco. This she did, even though the newborn had just come home from the ICU after having complications at birth.

Were they treating my husband different because they didn't like me?

Were they treating me different because they didn't like my husband?

My husband and I saw shows in Paris, walked the streets, and really enjoyed each other's company. I wish I knew we wouldn't have too many of more opportunities to be together in this way.

We went on to London. We were happy. We were in a good place in our marriage. Life has ups and downs. We were in our up. Our relationship was solid. We understood each other. We loved each other. We had always loved each other. We were in peace with one another.

In London, one day my husband and I were separated and I rode by myself in a taxi with my husband's mother, sister, brother, and Favorite Daughter-in-law. My husband's mother made a funky statement about the apartment bought decades ago in Iran. You know, the one I had made a bike analogy about.

She said, *you are lucky I bought that apartment for you because blah blah blah.* I stopped her and said you did not buy us that apartment. We bought it ourselves. You may be confused because you did buy one for your other son.

Favorite Daughter-in-law immediately gave her two cents. How she is sick and tired of me being so jealous of her. I gave her my four cents, don't give yourself so much credit dear. This has nothing to do with you. This has to do with my husband's mother and her false statement.

We arrived at our destination. Dirty looks at me were galore. My husband was confused as to what had happened in the short taxi ride. Our destination was the cemetery where my husband's cousin was buried. I knew his cousin well, better than my husband's siblings did. We had spent two weeks in London when our two older kids were just babies. My husband had to travel for work and I joined him on the trip and hung out with his cousin. Years later, she died an untimely death from cancer.

The tension in the cemetery was palpable as his family gathered on the side talking about money. Money money money is what this family talks about and maintains controls with.

My dad also talks about money, a different kind of talking though. My dad's talking is always sharing so others can make money the way he did. My husband's father has an income in the United States, thanks in part to my father and his talking about money. My father grew up with difficult circumstances, and is proud to have made a good life in California from a small town in Iran. With my husband's family, talk about Money was not positive. It was always a tool to show love and to show how you are not loved.

We went back to the rented London home, with my husband by my side. My husband's family wanted a family meeting. That was their thing, let's all have a meeting where we can gang up and be abusive as a group.

One particularly notable family meeting occurred when my husband and I had missed going to a party. The following morning they all showed up at our home wanting to find out what I had done to make their son not show up. I was the guilty one of course and it would be something I had done. They were fishing for some kind of weakness in our marriage and left disappointed. I was so frustrated. Who does that? Who shows up as a gang to your home to find out why you didn't go to a party the night before?

My mom had been in the hospital that night. My husband had not answered their phone calls but they didn't get a clue that he didn't want to go to the party. And to think that evening, I took the high road on behalf of my husband and, against his will, brought a gift for my husband's sister's boyfriend and briefly showed up for his birthday dinner.

On this particular occasion in London, I told my husband that their stupid family meetings where they came hunting for me, the witch, were ridiculous. I explained what the issue was this time.

Your mother said she bought us our apartment in Iran.
She clearly did not.
What the heck do we need a meeting for?

The meeting included me, my husband, my husband's father, mother, sister, brother, and Favorite Daughter-in-law. I had always liked and been kind to my husband's sister. I was blindsided with what happened next. She was acting like a police officer, interrogator, judge, and jury convinced that the target, me, was guilty.

Guilty of what?

Guilty of trust.

It was one of the most abusive interactions that I have had in my life. I kept looking at my husband and I think he was in pure shock.

> *You are not trustworthy.*
Are you saying you don't trust me?
Am I wrong? Did your mother buy the Tehran apartment for us or did we buy it?
> *You are just after our money.*
What is your proof of this?
I married for love.
Your brother didn't even have a working car when we met.
I bought our first home. I worked while he was in school.
We built our lives together outside of your family's influence, Ms. Trust Fund Baby who never had to build a life.
Ms. Mother-in-law who just married a rich older man.
What makes you think I'm after anything of yours not built?

The Herd looked at each other knowingly like they had a shared secret.

What is your smoking gun that you are hiding?
What is your proof that makes me untrustworthy?
What is your reason for hating on me?
Spill it, so we can get back to facts about who bought the apartment.

Out came the most ridiculous smoking gun I had ever heard.

My husband's sister, the facilitator of this meeting, said that the reason I'm untrustworthy is that her grandmother had claimed that I had cried because my husband was paying the expenses for his brother!

How does one respond to nonsense?

Her grandmother was a lovely lady who adored me.

Her grandmother had given me most of her family heirlooms including her wedding ring, knowing I would care for and pass them down to the next generation.
Her grandmother acknowledged that I had true love with her grandson.
Her grandmother would have long conversations with me apologizing for her daughter's behavior towards me.
Her grandmother would tell me stories of my husband's mother's younger days, her dad's militaristic attitude, and how she thought that was why her daughter was not at peace today.
Her grandmother, may she rest in peace.
Her grandmother was no longer with us to verify their smoking gun story.

Should one reply to nonsense?
Should one ignore the nonsense and dig deep to ask about their sufferings?

My husband's mother's mother, her grandmother, had asked me about my sufferings. I had shared how I found it difficult to connect with her daughter, my husband's mother. I had shared my observation that love and favoritism is shown with money in their family.

There was truth to a part of their smoking gun story, I did cry in the presence of my husband's grandmother. She had viewed my husband's brother's wedding album. Later she mentioned something to me that I myself had already noticed. In the sibling pictures, my husband had not been included.

I started to cry.
I cried for my husband.
I cried because I had been told there is no need for me to attend this wedding.
I cried because I made an effort to be inclusive of everyone at my own wedding.

My husband and I couldn't stop looking at each other. Seriously, in what universe did I cry because my husband is paying the expenses of his brother?

And let's assume this is true and "evil me" cried over money. Is this your proof of my untrustworthiness?

I refocused and asked again on behalf of my husband and I for the one-hundredth time. Did we or did we not buy the apartment in Iran? My husband's father finally spoke after an hour of my torturing and said, *it is true you sent money to Iran to buy this apartment.* I said, we are done here.

My husband, for the first and last time, stood up to his family in front of me. *You have no idea who my wife is. She doesn't even know her own business income. She doesn't care about money like you all do.*

My husband's sister had the last word saying *if this is true and your wife doesn't care about our money, she needs to prove herself to us.*

Was she stupid?
Was she a bitch?
Was she a stupid bitch?

After two decades of being with my husband, your brother, you never took the care to find out who I am and now it is my responsibility to "prove" myself to you?

I wonder, where do these selfish people come from?
I wonder, where do these self-centered people come from??
I wonder, where do these self-consumed people come from???

What is this fear for power?
What is this fear for control?
What is this fear for fabricating rightness to defend one's egos?

I later discovered how people of fear mirror and project. I had missed this my entire life. Anything that came out of their mouth had been their own demons reflected onto me.

How could I have missed this?
They are untrustworthy and they project it onto me.
They are materialistic and they project it onto me.
They are jealous and they project it onto me.

Favorite Daughter-in-law, in a moment of compassion, told me to ignore all they say and do. *Don't take it to heart.*

I, in a moment of crudeness, asked her if I should ignore all she had been to me as well?

The time you called me crying, before you were married, to say my husband's brother was cheating on you. I tell you what I would have told my own sister. Dump him. He is not into you. You will find someone who adores you. You turned it around into how I didn't want the two of you to be together and get married.

The time you wanted to see the emerald necklace my husband's mother had gifted me for the birth of my son. Then had the audacity to put into words that since you are marrying her favorite son, I should wait and see what she is going to gift you when you have a child.

The time you asked me how much my wedding dress, wedding ring, and wedding reception cost because you needed to receive the same or better. I explained to you that my wedding costs were shared. Take your focus off of my wedding costs and instead focus on what you like. You didn't even understand what I was saying and needed to find out what grade of diamond I had.

The time you decided that since you are married now and I own a home you have to own an equivalent home. You came over to verify how many bathrooms my home had. You told me that you have to have the same. I told you this is our second home. Both my husband and I worked and built our lives through time. You don't have to have the same as what I have now. You can build your life yourself and in time will be able to appreciate it more. That got turned around to how I'm jealous that my husband's parents are buying a home for the two of you.

The time my husband and I stopped by your house to wish you a happy birthday during your first year in the United States and unknowingly walked into a full on birthday party with mutual friends in attendance.

The time you loudly laughed and made fun of my family friend, the Baker's daughter, because she was overweight. And my embarrassment of standing next you when I realized she heard your mean fat comments.

The time my husband's brother needed something and the two of you stopped by to pick it up. As an exhausted young mother who had to transport my son to soccer practice with my sick toddler and baby in each hand, I, in my moment of need, got myself to ask you for a favor. I asked you if you would please give my son a ride to soccer on your way back home. You said *NO*. My husband's brother stepping in to say that of course he'd help.

The time that broke my heart the most was when my six-year-old son walked into your kitchen and politely asked you for a glass of water. Instead of simply giving him a glass of water, you stood there calling out for your husband to come into the kitchen so you could inform him that his nephew would like a glass of water. Not having a heart of service for a child is heartbreaking to me.

In a moment of vulnerability, Favorite Daughter-in-law apologized to me. Saying she was weak then. Now she is a mother and her focus and life has changed because of her son. I thought that perhaps she had not acted out of ill-intent after all.

We all prepared to go to the anniversary dinner. My husband's sister told me in a derogatory tone that they, the Herd, don't understand what my husband could possibly see in me. I ate my words. They are too blind to ever see what my husband saw in me. Instead, I just ignored her.

I told my husband's father you never have seen me as a part of your family. If you had, you all wouldn't treat me the way you do.

He refuted my statement. Insisting that I am a part of their family. As his wife stood next to him giving me her classic dirty look.

What was it about me that was so hateful for her?
What was it about me that was so hateful for them?

Was it because her son loved me?
Was it because her son chose to love me?

Or was it just about them and not me?
They hated themselves.
They couldn't see others happy.
They saw themselves as less than.
They had to act superior for their own survival.

My conclusion, it was about them and not me.

I didn't want to bring the anniversary gift to dinner. My husband convinced me to take the high road as he always did with his unique family. So I did. I brought the gift. I might add the only gift of the evening. To my surprise, my husband's sister, brother, and Favorite Daughter-in-law hadn't thought of doing anything for the anniversary couple that has done so much for their livelihood.

Even though they made us get up and go to the end of the table at the restaurant, I still stood up on that anniversary dinner and gave the speech I had written a month before. I gave them the gift of our children in a frame. It was one of the hardest moments in my life to put on a smile and praise people who have abused me.

I did it for love.
I did it for my husband.
I took his high road.

The next day, my husband and I were ready to have fun in London. I had some errands to run. Okay, buying bras from Marks and Spencer is a must when in London. We wanted to go on the London Eye together and experience the ride by ourselves now that we were kid-free.

I couldn't believe it. My husband's mother had the audacity to tell my husband, your wife can run her own errands come with us to a café and hang out. My husband said *NO*. He let them know we are sightseeing if they'd like to join us. Of course they did not. My heart broke on behalf of my husband.

One of the most fun days we had together was in London.
On the Eye and on the river ride.
We laughed.
We focused on ourselves.
We joked about what he could possibly see in me.
He knew he was loved by me.
I knew I was loved by him.
We both realized we lived authentic lives.

We both knew how blessed we were with our kids.
He knew our kids and I were his soul family.
He had known from day one I was his soul mate.

I am grateful.
I am grateful we were never in that family portrait.
I am grateful for sitting afar in restaurants.
I am grateful we were our own family unit and not under Herd influence.

How fortunate I am.
How loved I am.
How protected I am.

Chapter Eleven
Spring Visit

*To see oneself weaved with God
in a wildflower.*

Apologize.

I was wrong to say what I said.
I was wrong to do what I did.
I want to make it right.
I want to have a positive relationship with you.

I expected the Herd to act like I would have acted. That is
what I would tell someone if I realized I had been hurtful.
Could it be that they hadn't even realized what they had done?
It was so simple. Had they realized this and just apologized, I
would have been putty in their hands.

Where there is no remorse, there is no relationship.

Following the visit for their son's funeral, my husband's
parents had gone back to Iran. I was envisioning peace.

I had envisioned they would come back from Iran and we
would have one of their favorite family meetings. This time
with a facilitator that would listen to both sides. Then my
husband's family will realize and show remorse. From that
point on I will know to set boundaries such as my kids having
dinner with my husband's siblings only once a month.

I couldn't be furthest from the truth. Facilitators are for
conflict resolutions and not bullying situations. Any remorse
was a delusion on my part. At their core, they care more
about themselves, their power, and how others view them than
their grandchildren.

I started to study bullying behaviors.
I started to realize mine was a classic case of Family Bullying.
I started to study setting boundaries.
I started to study taking one's power back.

With my husband's parents gone.
With my husband's siblings ignoring me.
So came my downtime.

I could finally breathe.

I started to feel deep peace.
I started to navigate how I would heal.
I started to navigate how my kids would heal.
I started to have spurts of clarity in my mind of fog.

I started to begin to process what had happened.
And there was so much.

I had lost my husband.
I was heartbroken and needed emotional help to make sense
of it all.

I had lost my financial backing.
I was confused and needed to understand how my kids and I
would survive.

I had lost my health.
I was weak and needed help to tend to my health. I needed
strength in order to tend to my kids' health.

My son was organizing his dad's computer and found some
text exchanges between my husband and his sister. These
texts stated how upset she was that I was joining my husband
on our infamous last trip to Paris and London. How if I'm
going to be there, my husband's brother and his wife must be
there too. Also, creepy texts trying to entice my husband to
travel with her, without his kids and wife, to Greece. My
husband responded that his kids and wife are his only choice
and that his wife was not her competition.

Over and over again, I discover how smart my husband was.
Did his texts show that he had a clue about his sister's mind?
Since I was clueless, I had wanted to buy an extravagant gift
for her marriage contract acknowledgment. My husband did
not agree. I had tried so hard to convince my husband that we
should at least give his sister the same level gift for her
marriage that we had given to his brother years before.

I was so elated that my husband agreed to buy the same level gift for his sister. That gift, I never gave to my husband's sister.

My husband's brother sent a text to my son. *Bring your sisters and come to my home for a BBQ.* My son asked me if we are all going. I told my son I was not informed of this event. I believe your Uncle meant to only invite you and your sisters. My son, at 18 years of age, understood what my husband's brother in his 40 plus years of age did not. It was wrong to ask my son to bring his sisters over without asking for parental consent, meaning my consent.

What was my husband's brother thinking to place that kind of pressure on a young adult who had just lost his father? *Your mother should be disregarded. We are interested mainly in you and then your sisters.*

Or was he thinking?
My kids had just lost their father.
Their world was upside down.
The only person left for them was their mother.

If he really cared for my kids, he would realize this.
If he really cared for my kids, he would act with my kids' best interest in mind.
If he really cared for my kids, he would understand that real caring is selfless.

I knew my husband's parents would come back to the United States for the spring equinox as they have traditionally in the years past.

My home phone rang and it was my husband's father. After pleasantries were exchanged welcoming them back to the States, he made a point to tell me that my son did not return his phone call. He suggested that I had instructed my son to not return his call. I ignored his unsubstantiated claim. I was informed that they wish to see my son. That was the purpose of his phone call to me, to get my son to visit them.

My son did visit them.
They had brought him gifts.
My husband and his parents had always been and are generous gift givers.

While grateful for all the gifts bestowed upon him, my son was troubled. Why did they only ask him to go? How can they give such importance to him and overlook his sisters? Are they playing favoritism in his generation? My son knew his father's brother was a favorite, even when his father was alive.

My husband's mother called me that evening. She was very kind on the phone. I welcomed them back to the States. My heart aches for my husband's mother. No matter what our past, no mother should survive her child.

My husband's mother asked why the girls and I did not stop by with my son. I told her because it was very clear that only my son was requested. She wanted to make peace; that came across loud and clear in her tone. She then invited my kids and me to their home for the Spring Equinox Dinner.

For years, because my husband's parents lived in Iran and only visited for a limited time, my birth family was gracious enough to give up time with us for this special traditional dinner.

Now I did not have my husband.
I was ever heartbroken by his family.
I was learning to set my boundaries.

I told her that we had other plans.

NO MORE. That life of them saying jump and us cancelling other plans was gone.

It was time to keep plans with my own parents, siblings, and their children.
It was time to be with my birth family who has had my back throughout my ordeal.
I was not willing to share anymore.
I was not willing to share with people who despise me.

Out of compassion, I offered to visit my husband's mother with my kids for the Persian New Year.

So I did. I called them the day of the spring equinox. I made plans to go visit them, as is customary for the first day of spring. I felt unsafe visiting them. My parents, who would have visited independent of me, joined me for support.

I had one last gift for my husband's mother. Another framed picture –a picture of my husband. One last push, here was your son. The son you could have been grateful to and for.

We sat in their home.
I felt rage overcome me for the way my husband and I had been treated.
Not only after my husband died also for all the decades before.

My husband's mother wanted to be kind.
I would not accept.
I could not accept.

There had been no acknowledgement of how poorly they had treated me.
There had been no acknowledgement of how remorseful they were.
There had been no acknowledgement that they wanted a positive relationship with me.

Being nice once doesn't mean anything anymore.
It has been their typical behavior. Reel me in so they can attack again.
What had changed? Nothing when there is no genuinely stated remorse.

I was cold.
I was distant.
I made the bare minimum conversation.

My own mother filled the space talking about this and that, as is typical of her sweet loving soul that wants to create a space of peace.

My husband's mother talked about the services held for my husband in Iran. How her favorite son gave the best speech ever. "You should have been there to experience it", she said. It was videotaped. She could share the video and pictures with us.

Suddenly, this disgust feeling of Favorite Daughter-in-law's laughter and selfies taken on the day of my husband's funeral overcame my mind. I lashed out at my husband's mother unfairly. Or was it untimely?

My husband has passed away and you want to share pictures and videos with me? To remember what? I gave her a piece of my mind as harshly as a non-validated heartbroken person would.

Really, what I was saying is that I have never seen the reason that your son and Favorite Daughter-in-law take a thousand pictures a day of themselves and their children. I can't understand how they didn't have the sensitivity to include my husband in their wedding sibling pictures. How the Herd could take a family portrait and not include my husband, their son. Really, what I was saying is I don't get the insensitivity of Favorite Daughter-in-law's loud laughter and selfies on my husband's funeral day.

LOVE can save lost souls.
I was drained and did not have it in me to offer that love.

I was ready to leave.
As we were leaving, my husband's father reached to hand me the gift of a gold coin.

Couldn't he see that kindness is a far more valuable currency than gold?
Couldn't he see that our souls get weary under the weight of gold?

Traditionally, for the celebration of spring, they would generously gift us gold coins.

I did not want to accept the gift.
How can you be so abusive, using money as a tool of power, only to turn around and give such a generous gift?
I wanted to say keep it now so I don't have to return it later.
I wanted to say keep it so I pay forward for the gift money I'm suppose to return to you.
I didn't.
Instead I ended the awkward interaction. I said that I would accept it for my kids.

I didn't want the energy of that gift
I didn't need the energy of that gift.

All my broken heart needed then was acknowledgement of poor treatment.
All my broken heart needed then was remorsefulness.
All my broken heart needed then was stated positive intent in our relationship.

All I needed was to stop feeling guilty because I was not nice to them during my visit.
It felt foreign to be so cold and full of rage.
I didn't like myself for what had transpired.

I asked the universe an important question.
What is the purpose in all that has occurred for me?

The universe gave me an important answer.
I must learn to be kind to myself.
I must accept myself where I am.
I must remember that no matter what, I am LOVE.

My husband's mother called to thank me for the picture of her son I had gifted her. Her kindness of heart came through the phone.

She asked about my son's college choice and how I am planning to support him for college. I was matter-of-fact. He had not heard from all the schools, so he has not made a choice. She indicated that they wanted to help. I told her that I don't need their kind of twisted help. Her husband had already made it very clear that he wanted an account to be opened that was funded by my father yet managed by him. I do not need my husband's father to manage any accounts for me. I just need him to do the right thing and return my kids' existing educational accounts to me.

She then went on to say that her husband was wrong to not return educational accounts to me. The money that my husband earned in his lifetime belonged to my kids and me.

Was this being remorseful or taking personal responsibility? She is talking about her husband's actions and her daughter's statement.

I was as rudely snide as one can be. I said thank you for that, now I can see why the gift money you gave us belongs to you because my husband did not earn it.

She went on to say how the gift money was for her son and his family, my kids and I. She explained how my husband initially did not accept the gift and it was she who pushed her son to accept the $100,000. My husband's mother said of course it should not be returned. Gifts should never be returned to the originator.

Where was her change of heart coming from?
Was it temporary or would it sustain?

As I was listening, I thought, she is right. It was always impossible for my husband to accept monetary gifts. My husband did not accept monetary gifts from my parents either. I would tell him how rude it was when he turned down a gift. People show love with gifts and you are not accepting their love. He corrected me that quality time was a better gift of love.

My husband's brother had gifted us $1,000 for our new home. My husband had not cashed that check. Upon his death, I returned the $1,000 check back to my husband's brother. I could have easily deposited it in the bank and moved on. I returned the money to honor my husband's request of no acceptance. Was this the portal that gave the right to my husband's brother to ask for his parents' gift back from me? Did he not see the return I had made was to honor my husband? Did he think that if I return his gift, I must now return his parents?

The conversation took us to what happened the night I kicked my husband's brother and sister out of my home.

This is where I failed myself. There was so much that happened that night. It took me months to find the heart of my issue with my husband's siblings.

At the core of it, I was upset and shocked that my husband's sister claimed that my husband was untrustworthy and had stolen money. The fact that she had the capacity to talk about money only one day after her brother's death still has me in disbelief.

Instead my reply to my husband's mother focused on how my husband's sister is saying I'm untrustworthy and I will want to steal my own money set aside for my own kids. First of all, who in the world is able to steal their own money? Second, is she insulting my motherhood? How dare she. She has no clue what it takes to Build a life. Build a marriage. Build a family.

She chooses to insult the institution of marriage. Let's have a "Signing Papers Party" instead of a wedding? We will sign papers so that we are married on paper. However, he can continue living in Los Angeles and I will continue living here.

Why mock marriage?
There is nothing wrong with having the belief that there is no need to get married. If you do, then Don't.
Don't get married.
Don't mock the sanctity of marriage and what it stands for.

My humbled husband's mother then started to tell me how in the midst of her hatred for me, she knew I was the best of mothers. Did she tell me in the midst of her hatred for me? Yeah she did.

My husband's mother also wanted me to know that she wanted to leave an inheritance for my kids. I told her I want to do a lot of things in life too. Getting things done is a different story. Still, my heart understood and accepted my husband's mother's remorsefulness for her own words.

She then wanted to make sure I am not bad mouthing the Herd to my kids. Telling my kids lies to turn them against the Herd as she had envisioned it. For a moment, it occurred to me, does she speak from experience? Did she say lies about me to turn her husband and kids against me? I explained to her that I would never do that. I'm not and have never been her enemy. She is her own enemy. Instead of worrying about what I would say and do, she should worry about what she and her Herd say and do.

Her vulnerability softened me. I broke down and asked her how she was holding up. I must say it has never occurred to anyone from my husband's birth family to ask me that question. How are you holding up? Forget about what can we do for you. Just, how are you holding up? How are your kids holding up?

She told me she was in a lot of physical pain. How a bus had hit her while crossing the street in Iran. My heart dropped for her. I have experienced physical pain.
I offered to take her to my younger sister, the Chiropractor.
She refused me.
I offered to cup her to reduce her aches and pain.
She refused me.
I offered to take her to my shaman acupuncturist.
She refused me.

Was she not able to accept my love in the form of healing?
Or does her intellectual ego live in fear of my mysticism?
I dropped the subject and did not make any more offers.

I mentioned to her how I had dreamt about my husband and how he had told me that my husband's mother needed him and he must go to her. Maybe he was there to protect her from something worse that could have happened from being hit by that bus. She then said that she had had the same dream about her son.

I thought, did she really have the same exact dream as I?

181

Then I thought, is this just a repeat of the past? When I have an experience to proclaim, she has to match the experience or up it as if it were poker.

Our long conversation came to an end.

My husband's mother had a rough childhood, as conveyed to me by her own mother. She needed to have control of situations for her sanity. How can I ever truly know what it's like to wear her shoes? She lived through the heart-wrenching Iran vs. Iraq war. She survived the ups and downs of a life lived. I have seen her love. I have experienced her love. I know her love. I just no longer wish to experience her hate.

A week later, my husband's father called. In a derogatory tone, as if he had no choice but to make the wrong decision and transfer my kids' educational accounts to me, he asked me to meet him at the brokerage firm the next morning. I told him I would not. I had plans at that time. I informed him that I would call him back and let him know when I was available.

For over two decades my husband had a tendency to always drop whatever plans we had if they said jump. This, in my husband's mind, was a sign of respect for his parents. I could not follow his tradition for people who had been so abusive to me. I will honor my life. I will not drop my other plans just because they want me to jump.

I know change is hard. I understand that powerful people who are used to having what they want when they want it, don't like to hear *No*.

I know that men of Fear need to have perceived power.
I know that men of Power have courage of vulnerability.

I called my husband's father the following week and gave him two time choices for a meeting with the brokerage firm. It became very clear it was either the time he says or no time at all. It had nothing to do with availability and everything to do with perceived power.

Wow, this was part of the textbook bullying behavior I was learning about. The person who bullies will not allow their victim to pick the location and time of their encounter. The bully always determines the place and time, never giving a choice.

I agreed to his time. I was cognizant of what he had just done to maintain power over me. I asked my son to join me at the brokerage firm because I did not want to be alone with my husband's father.

My son and I were late and walked into the consultant's office, joining my husband's sister and father. My husband's sister turned her head and did not say hello to me. My son took notice of this behavior.

The consultant was explaining the transfer of accounts. I realized that my husband's sister was not translating properly for my husband's father. I took over this responsibility and started to translate for him. In the midst of my kindness, he did not hesitate to attack. He had the audacity to ask the consultant what precautions can be taken so that I do not spend my kids' educational funds for myself. My son was shocked to witness this encounter.

The transfer and meeting couldn't have ended any sooner. We walked into the lobby of the brokerage firm. I told my husband's father, you treat me this poorly because you do not see me as part of your family. My husband's sister chimed in to say *STOP — you are dis-respecting my father.*

I am disrespecting?
Look in the mirror at all you have been.

Look in the mirror at all you have all been.

My son and I left.
My son was in disbelief at what he had just witnessed.
My son elevated this primal instinct of having to protect his mother.

I explained to my son. It is irrelevant how badly they treated me. It is important that we got your accounts back. Let's keep our focus on moving our lives forward.

That was the theme of my year as my soul was void of hope and my *beingness* was empty of life.

Focus.
Focus on moving my life forward.
Focus on moving my kids' lives forward.
Focus on continuing to live so we can start living again.

My husband's father calls. In a derogatory tone, he says *have your son bring me your property tax bill and I will go to the Tax Collector office with your son to pay it.*

Again I'm at a loss of words at the savageness guised in helpfulness comment.

What is his intention?
What is his motivation?

Is he offering to pay my property taxes?
Do I tell him that my tax bill had already been paid by my older sister to relieve me of worries during this difficult time?
Do I tell him that this is public record? Anyone with an Internet connection can look up with a simple address search?
Do I tell him that if you had the wits to go to my brokerage firm and find out exactly how much I have in my kids' accounts, I have to believe you have done a simple Internet check of public records to find out if and when my tax bill was paid?

I didn't even know how to reply to him.
I wasn't sure how I could make it clear that I'm not playing their games.
I am not playing any games.
Leave me the fuck alone.

Could it be so he can tell others he offered to help?
Could it be he really doesn't know it has already been paid?
Could it be that he really wants to help?

Seriously, if he really wanted to help he would have done just that, *help*. Without strings attached. The whole conversation felt dirty. Did he want to *buy* my son? Was his plan to catch me, an untrustworthy and money hungry person, in the act of lying? Was that his attempt to bring my son to 'his' side? Why are they so fixated on wanting to portray me as a liar? What is this silly Witch Hunt?

I replied the way they used to answer my husband when my husband would ask to spend time with them. I said, let's wait and see what happens. How my husband hated that answer from them. Let's wait and see what happens.

I had my husband's father so confused. He never expected his words to his son out of my mouth to him. Really, they haven't expected much of what they have seen out of me. I have valor. They had been blind to this fact.

My husband's family has always been confused about me. I look Persian. I speak Persian, though not very well. I am Persian in heritage. I am not Persian in my living. In my heart, I have always been and am American. I have never understood nor cared for the Persian cultural intricacies. In all fairness to my husband's parents, it is hard to see a duck quack like a duck yet know it is not a duck.

185

Is it society or was it just my husband's family? There are many who are also confused about people of generous heart. Instead of realizing these people are people of strength and people so evolved to give unconditional love, they are viewed as weak people. People ripe to be stepped on. I know because I have been witness to my mom. Her strength. Her love. I have also seen her unconditional love misunderstood for weakness.

Can't a woman be generous of heart and strong combined?
I am generous of heart and strong.
I love myself enough to verbalize it.

My younger daughter's birthday was approaching and regardless of my husband's father's ruthless treatment, I invited my husband's parents to her family birthday party. I did not invite my husband's sister nor brother. Why would I?

I strongly felt my only moral commitment was to my husband's parents, as my children's grandparents. I would make every effort for them to have their grandchildren in their lives. My husband's siblings would have to ask to spend time with my kids. Which they had not.

Do I love my husband's brother's children? Yes, I love all children. Did it break my heart that I felt I could not have my husband's brother's children at my younger daughter's birthday party? Yes, because I want my children to care for and know all their cousins.

But I know better.
When there is no relationship with the parent, there is no relationship with the child.
When there is no contact, there is no relationship.
When there is no remorse, there is no relationship.

By now, four months had passed since all the abusive behavior. Not once was there an outreach from my husband's siblings asking:

How are you holding up?
We are sorry for what happened.
We want to see your kids.
We want a positive relationship with you and your kids.

My husband's parents came to my younger daughter's
birthday party. As always they brought the most generous gift
for my younger daughter. The first thing they said to me was
in the words of my husband's brother's son "Hap Bitday."

I realized something in that moment. I realized that my
husband's parents' anchor was their Herd— my husband's
brother, his wife, and my husband's sister.

They need their Herd for survival.
They need their Herd for breath.
They need their Herd for life.
Without their Herd, they feel powerless in my presence. Why
was that? Why can't they, after two decades, just make peace
with me in their lives?

My heart went to my husband's mother as she unknowingly
alienated her grandson. Putting out in the open the concept of
money with strings attached. Putting out in the open that a
relationship with them will be one of control where they tell
you what to do and you have to obey. The very opposite of the
kind of healthy relationships of mutual understanding that my
son knows and lives.

> *If you go to the university back East, we will pay for
> your education. If you stay in California, we will not.*
My son replied that he felt the need to stay in California.

His father had passed away.
He needed to stay close to his sisters and me.
He realized that need and was respecting it.

Then came the comments. *You want to stay close to your mother and become a mama's boy? You have to go far away to become a man.* My son did not cave in.

Then came the comments to me. *This is because of money. You are stifling him because you can't afford a private university.*

I replied: Ultimately, what your son, my husband, wanted and how we brought up our children is to make their own life decisions. I will not dare influence or make a life decision for my child. Let's be grateful that we are giving to society a mature person of tremendous worth.

If he wants to be in California now, I shall support him. He can always leave the state in pursuit of graduate work.

Please be joyous for him.
Please be joyous for us.
Please join me in supporting him.

They hated being at my younger daughter's birthday party as had I hated visiting them for the first day of spring. I understood. I had worn the same shoes. Still, when they left I felt displeased with my inability to make a better experience for them as guests in my home.

I looked in the mirror to see what I can do different. I thought, I should have them over without anyone else around so that they are able to bond by spending quality time with their grandchildren.

I kept a positive focus. I called and invited my husband's parents to come and see their grandchildren. They did. They came and saw my younger daughter's soccer game and took my kids out to ice cream. One thing I did notice, they did not wish to come into my home.

My heart fueled with empathy for my husband's parents.
Living in fear.
Protecting themselves from their own vulnerabilities.

Fearing the unknown.
Fearing the now.
Fearing the light.

Is it so important what others think and say?
Can there be freedom from living life based on other's judgments?
Can there be peace in loving oneself?
Can there be peace in the courage to be true to oneself?

The advantage of culture helps.
What happened to China has now happened to Iran.

When communists took over China, they ousted the high caliber people of China. They favored and promoted those who were animalistic in behavior. This was a cultural coup d'Etat. The same is true of Iran post-revolution. It scares me that in the United States a podium has now been provided for animalistic behavior.

I shall never take for granted that I live in a hotbed of spiritual growth.
I shall never take for granted that I live in a hotbed of trust.
I shall never take for granted that I live in a hotbed of respect.

I was on a plane going to Iran with my toddler son and baby older daughter. The three of us were fast asleep as we generally are on trains, planes, and automobiles.

I had always considered myself an easy traveller. I fall asleep only to wake up for bathroom breaks and upon arrival.

When I went on my first cruise with my husband and three young children. I recall taking a nap.

189

I opened my eyes to say thank you to my husband who was managing all three children. I opened my eyes to a very upset husband who was dragging me out of bed.

I was asking him to let me take a nap. What are you doing?
You have been asleep for over 33 hours.
That can't be. I am only taking a nap.

We went to the ship doctor to find out that I have motion sickness. One pill and I was manageably fine for the rest of that trip— the last cruise of my life.

On that plane ride to Iran, another mother came up to me and asked me for some pills. I didn't understand her. She thought I had pills that I had given to my children to have them sleep. She wanted some. I thought, Lady, giving drugs to your perfectly healthy and happy baby is called child endangerment.

I told her I fall asleep easily and my children follow suit. She insisted that I'm lying. I have pills that I don't want to share with her. I told her I have been tired before with the overwhelming task of taking care of a baby. Your baby wants to play, let me help you. I can hold and play with your baby to give you some time off.

She just gave me a dirty look and walked away.

Now I wonder, is this the new culture of Iran?
Or should I ask, is this the old culture of humanity?

Take a pill, use alcohol or drugs to not deal with living life.
Assume others are lying to you and are ill intended.
Do not trust help offered or love shown because there has to be an ulterior motive.

My husband's sister sent an email titled "122 days of unending grief."

This unfortunate situation has gone on for too long. We are all weary and sad and our lives have changed forever. Being harsh to one another is not helping our kids who need to grow up in the heart of kindness and bonded families. Our take on life, our approach towards disasters, our patience and understanding for the unexpected, even the way we show and announce our love, might be well different on our side of family compared to yours, but that doesn't change the fact that we all love "him" equally and unconditionally and that this grief is a shared grief.

We have to make sure our children receive the love and warmth they deserve after their father left them too early. My ask is to surround them with love and not with bitterness and distance, each family to its own ways. Your ways and expectations might be (and definitely is) different from ours, but it doesn't make either of us wrong, just, well, different.

If you can try to accept us the way we are and we can accept you the way you are, we can have the relationship that our children deserve, making sure there's no animosity and anger, which at this point I am certain is caused by our unending grief.

A lot needs to be forgiven, and if not possible, forgotten. There are no winners when you start looking for people to blame. I am sure each family considers itself in the right but at this point we just have to look past it. As my parents, brother and I love to see our beautiful children move forward in life, you should also want to have your husband's original small family present in his children's milestones.

Let me know if your thoughts are in line with what I have just said and we'll take it from there.

Hope you are well,

I received this email and was pleasantly touched by the outreach.

I read this email and knew this was a monumental move for my husband's sister. She took the first step of outreach toward someone she sees as inferior.

I recognize that my husband's sister made an effort to spend time with my kids and be present in their lives prior to her brother's/my husband's passing.

I read this email again and my ego felt offended.

I read this email over again.
I asked myself was my husband's sister trying to apologize?
No. She was not.

I read this email yet again.
I asked myself was she putting me in a position to defend myself?
Yes. She was.

It caught my eye that she said all this is caused by "unending grief".
Is it really? Did you treat me well prior to my husband's passing?

It caught my eye that she surfaced the concept of "being different".
Doesn't she know the number one excuse of a person with bullying behavior is to blame differences instead of taking personal responsibility?

It caught my eye that she asked me to "accept us the way we are and we will accept you the way you are". What does that mean? I should accept their abusive behavior towards me? They will accept my frustration and yelling at them?

It caught my eye that she implied I'm raising my kids in an environment of bitterness and hate. How fortunate that they have now offered to come and save the day.

I was left with one burning question.
How was it my responsibility to make sure they will be present for my kids' milestones?

Last I checked, I am not the owner of milestones.
They know the time of my kids' milestones.
They can take responsibility to reach out to them.
They can send a card or gift in the mail.
They can call and wish them well-being.
They can call and ask to spend quality time with them.

Or, are milestones about showing one's face at a party that I must host, so pictures can be taken and posted on social media for validation from peers?

The most important person in the world will never be physically present for my kids' milestones. If my husband, my kids' dad, is not at a gathering what does it matter who else comes or doesn't come? Of what importance are the photos taken at a superficial party then?

I did what any sane person would do.
I shared this email with my Spiritual Friend for another set of eyes.

I did what any democratic mother would do.
I shared this email with my three kids.

I asked each one of us to write a reply.
We then would share our replies with each other and decide how we would proceed.

My reply with Spiritual Friend's insight: I don't recall anyone asking me to want to spend time with my kids and my rejecting the idea.

My son's reply: Delete email and do not waste your time with a reply.

My older daughter's reply: It is not healthy for us to move forward with any relationship unless the pattern of hostility towards our mother has been addressed.

My younger daughter's reply: They only care to see our milestones?

The five of us had a family tradition for our birthdays. On the night of our birthdays, we went out to dinner together. On a different evening, we would get together with our extended families to celebrate. It occurred to me how envious my husband's sister was about our tradition.

My husband's sister would call for my husband's birthdays, being assertive about joining the five of us for dinner. At times I would relent. I felt sorry for her never having lived with her brother under one roof. When she was a baby, her brother/my husband departed Iran. I saw it as an effort on her part to reconnect with a brother she never really knew.   I would tell her that she could join our family birthday dinner.

She still was never able to infiltrate our sacred tradition. My husband always stood up to her and wouldn't allow it.

We decided that my husband's sister's email contained too many micro-aggressions and missed two important factors.

Missing the need for acknowledgement of transgression.
Missing the need for remorsefulness.

This email was missing the most important factor of all.
Picking up the phone and calling to speak in person.
My son was right, the email was not worthy of a reply.

Textbook bullying.

Instead of taking responsibility for one's own behavior, blaming other factors. Instead of taking responsibility with personal contact, sending off an arrogant email.

The entire email placed me in a position of having to defend myself. I had now grasped that if one is placed under attack and made to justify oneself, one is dealing with a predatory situation. I'm learning that I never have to defend myself to predators.

There had been no contact from my husband's birth family. In good faith I called my husband's parents again to invite them over to my home for lunch the following week on a Wednesday. My kids did not have school. I figured this would provide plenty of quality time for grandparents and grandchildren to be together. I had planned to go upstairs and let them bond without my heartbroken energy in the middle. They could play card games in the comfort of our home.

Wednesday morning came. Pillar Friend had come over to help with grocery shopping and making lunch. Mid-morning, I received a text from my husband's father. *We will see you for dinner at so-and-so restaurant at 7 p.m.* I was dumbfounded. The plans were made for lunch at my home. I called my husband's father. I told him, I am confused we had plans for lunch today at my home. Why did you send a text for dinner out at a restaurant? My kids cannot come tonight. Two have soccer practice and one has tickets to see the Giants game with friends.

The conversation with my husband's father went south fast.

He started to attack me saying that I don't want them to see the children. I tried to explain, I'm the one who called you and made plans for you to come to my home for lunch and spend time with your grandchildren. My kids have plans tonight and cannot go out. I invited you a week ago for lunch. Why can't you come for lunch today? He attacked me again saying I was a liar. I am keeping the children away from them. Our plans were in fact for the evening at a restaurant.

I hung up in disbelief.
How will I tell my kids that their grandparents canceled and are not coming?
I was shaking from the unfounded attack.

Pillar Friend calmed me.
Pillar Friend suggested we go to their home and see them face-to-face.
Pillar Friend thought we could then bring them back with us to my home for the original plan of lunch and spending time with my kids.

We went over there.
It turned out that something better had come up.
Some of my husband's father's friends were going gambling and he was getting ready to go with them.

The fact that going gambling was more important than spending quality time with his grandchildren enraged me.

The fact that he blamed me for having the time wrong and didn't have the decency to say something better came up could we reschedule enraged me.

The fact that I had invited them and he was accusing me of keeping "the children" away from them enraged me.

I yelled at him.
Don't you care about your grandchildren?
Don't you want to see and be with your grandchildren?

My husband's mother chimed in.
>*With a mother like you, those children are not worth being with.*

My husband's mother's classic dirty look came back.
She just could not sustain being nice to me.

And then, in the most eloquent way, she took focus away from the core of our issue— spending time with their grandchildren.

She started yelling at me.
>*You are telling people I am responsible for my son's*
death.
I stop her.
I never made such a statement.
Who are "the people" you are claiming that I have said this to?
Let's call one of them now to verify while we are both standing here.

Seriously, she was the one who made the nasty comment to me about how I have something to hide because I didn't do an autopsy.

I yelled back at my husband's mother.
Give me the name of one person you claim I have made such a statement to.

My husband's mother did not have a name to give.
She just yelled back at me in English to "Get Out."

Get Out?
How long did you wait for that one?
Do you even know the abuse your living children and husband put me through that I had to kick them out of my home?

I gladly left after one Get Out.

Pillar Friend stayed back trying to make a bad situation better.

Pillar Friend came out to say they want to have a meeting with me and my parents to discuss what took place.

I told Pillar Friend, Absolutely Not.
I will never ever in my life again enter into their abusive family meetings where they want to overpower me and break me down with their lies.

It is straightforward.
I invited them for lunch today.
They decided to go gambling instead.

They had a choice to take responsibility for their change of heart in spending time with their grandchildren.

They had a choice to NOT enact a nonsensical attack that the plans were for tonight and I don't want my kids to see them.

They had a choice to NOT say with a mother like me, those children are not worth being with.

I made up my mind in that moment.
I will no longer push my kids on them.
If they want to see their grandchildren, they need to call me and ask for it.

Pillar Friend, in an effort to make peace, talked to my parents to see if they would be willing to have a meeting with my husband's parents to discuss issues. Independent of me, my parents made it clear they would not. They do not have any issues with their in-laws.

My parents comprehended their in-laws had lost their son, for they had lost the same son. My parents did not take to heart the lack of responsiveness and respect towards them by their in-laws. My parents were empathetic towards my husband's parents. My husband's parents had rejected my mom's outreach towards them. My husband's parents had not even repaid a spring equinox visit to my parents.

Before I was heartbroken, confused, and bewildered.
Now I was enraged.

My husband's parents did call a couple of weeks later, wanting
to see my kids.
I invited them to our home.
They insisted on a restaurant.

Though it was against the Protect Oneself from Bullying Rules,
my kids and I went.

My kids and I parked our car.
In walking to the restaurant, we saw Favorite Daughter-in-law
trying to calm her baby outside.

I thought to myself, how naïve of me.
Of course, it wouldn't have just been grandparents.
Of course, my husband's father would not keep our agreement
that I only deal with my husband's parents. My heart told me
to turn around and leave. I did not listen to my heart. I stayed
for the sake of my kids spending time with their grandparents.

I went up and initiated greetings with Favorite Daughter-in-
law and exchanged pleasantries. Taking note of her cheeky
response, I thought, why did I say hello first to her? She
should have said hello to me first.

I decided to hold my tongue when I got inside the restaurant.

We walked in and everyone was seated. The end of the table
was made available for me. The entire Herd was there.

Only my husband's father greeted me. No one else even said a
hello!! And neither did I. The atmosphere was awkward.

My husband's mother asked my son why he didn't return the
Herd's messages. My son replied that he didn't want to.

My husband's brother who had sent an Evite to my three kids for his daughter's birthday asked them if they would attend. Each one of my kids politely said they would not. I guess he didn't understand that not inviting their mother was a big deal to my kids.

My husband's sister was asking questions from my younger daughter who was seated next to her.

My husband's father was trying to make conversation with me about weather and other irrelevant matters. I was not interested in any dumb conversations.

In the middle of dinner, Favorite Daughter-in-law walked over to my side of the table and threw me a 'hello' as if she is such a big person to do so. As if I hadn't even said hello to her first outside the restaurant. I must be immune to her behavior because it no longer surprises me.

The worst part of the evening for me was when, with proudness, Favorite Daughter-in-law proclaimed how her one-year-old can be on her iPad for over 3 hours straight.

As if this is a badge of honor.
As if this makes the child a genius.
As if this makes her mother of the year.

My heart crushed for her child.
My heart judged it as child neglect.

I forgave myself for judging. In truth, I am not aware of how life should unfold for this young child.

I found empathy. Favorite Daughter-in-law is doing the best she knows how. I found clarity. My husband's brother does his best to compensate.

And then, the worst part of the evening became the most profound.

Why do they hate me so much?
It has to do with the kind of women we are.

It is a known truth among women that some are meant to be mothers. Some are not meant to be mothers.

Is it one's nature?
Is it nurture?

It is heartbreaking when a meant-to-be parent cannot have children.
It is disastrous when a not-meant-to-be parent has children.

Both categories are valid and necessary.

Is it that we decide who our parent will be prior to being born so that we learn the life lessons that we seek to learn?

Or is it that our collective evolution is in recognizing who we are and living true to our own being?

If we know we are meant to be a parent, we know it in our heart.
If we know we are not meant to be a parent, we know it in our heart.
Living your true living. Living your heart's calling.

I see how same-sex parents and parents who adopt against the odds are meant-to-be parents and know it in their hearts.

I now respect my husband's sister for knowing her truth and choosing to not have children. My husband's mother and her favorite daughter-in-law match. All three women fit the category of "disastrous when parent to a child".

I am a person of heart and know that any parent loves their child. No parent ever sets out to be disastrous in their responsibilities.

I am human. I am the first to admit that I made mistakes as a mother. However, I took my motherhood responsibilities professionally. I read books, listened to tapes, and attended speeches all in an effort to be the most successful parent I could be with the lives I had been gifted to guardian.

I had always known in my heart that I wanted to be a mother.
I had always known in my heart that I would be a mother.
I have always known in my heart that I love being a mother.

Had this been our divide?

Would I have tension if a woman, opposite to me, who was not meant to be a mother married my son? I cannot say. I can say there may be tension if such a hypothetical woman lacked self-awareness and decided to have children. And I also acknowledge that I cannot be the judge of any outcome, for I do not know God's plan.

God, while making plans, please keep in mind that my preference is for my son to marry a woman who is meant to be a mother. And God, please also know that I will promise an open heart of love either way.

I was so relieved when dinner was over. My body had been shaking practically the entire time. My son held my hand in an effort to stop the shaking. I thought, if I had known the entire Herd would be here I would have brought support, in the form of my older sister and her husband. We all got up to leave. I refused to say goodbye to anyone. Not that they were saying goodbye to me.

These people had been abusive. Why am I thinking they don't have the decency to recognize their offenses committed? They don't even have the decency to say hello or speak a word to me during the entire dinner experience.

My husband's mother realized we were en route to our car. Suddenly niceness overcame her. She caught up with me to say and give me a hug goodbye. What was I supposed to do with that? I said a cold goodbye and left. Why couldn't she have said one word to me the entire night at the restaurant?

What was the purpose of having me at dinner outside with the Herd?
Was it to seat me at the end of the table and be abusive for old time's sake?

Why couldn't my husband's parents just come to my home and spend quality time with their grandchildren? Play cards. Bond souls. Practice peace.

Why can they not understand that matters just got worse?
Why can they not see the difficult position this puts their grandchildren in?

Why can they not comprehend?
Why can I not comprehend?

People are not me.
People don't think like me.
People don't act like me.

On the car ride back, my younger daughter felt guilty. She felt like there were too many questions thrown her away and she had divulged too much information. We all reassured her that she is a new thirteen-year-old and it was the responsibility of the adult to not invade privacy. She should be proud of herself. She should be kind to herself. We have nothing to hide. There is no guilt in sharing, even when she felt pressured to.

My husband's sister discovered, from the information gathered from my younger daughter during dinner, that I would be out of town during the birthday party weekend. She texted my younger daughter, who was at a friend's house for a sleepover, to offer to pick her up and take her to her cousin's birthday party. My younger daughter immediately called me to inform me what had occurred.

My sisters had taken me to Los Angeles to attend an identity weekend seminar. This was to help move my life forward. It was planned by my older sister's childhood friend who had received her master's degree in Spiritual Psychology.

Spiritual Friend, my sisters, and I were having a great time connecting on an intimate level as we poured our souls out with laughter and joy. We were visited by a White Butterfly that all of us simultaneously believed to be my husband. My joy was cut short by this phone call and we returned home from Los Angeles within the day.

I was fed up with my husband's siblings bypassing me in order to get to my kids.
Didn't they get the message from my kids' responses or lack thereof?

For God's sake, I never contact my own sisters' kids to take them out without my sisters knowing and approving.

I sent my husband's siblings the following email.
An email to convey they cannot be predatory towards me any more.

> *When my younger daughter is solicited without parental consent or knowledge for transportation, not only is this act immoral, it is illegal.*
>
> *http://leginfo.legislature.ca.gov/faces/codes_displayS ection.xhtml?lawCode=PEN&sectionNum=272.*

This is a formal warning. Though I had chosen to ignore immoral behavior in the past, if required, I will take legal action in the future.

As a moral citizen, it is your responsibility to include and gain consent from parent of minors for the solicitation of meeting and transporting.

I said it.
I'm frustrated that you choose to disregard me over and over again.
I said it.
You are barking up the wrong tree.
I said it.
You are immoral per societal standards.

I got a phone call from my husband's father that they are traveling back to Iran. He wants my husband's passport and Iranian death certificate prior to his departure.

I called him back and said I'm not interested in providing any documents to him until I receive the original title to my apartment in Iran.
He called me back and said that his wife and he would like to come see the kids before they leave. I welcomed them. I gave them two time choices when all three kids would be available. He didn't like being given two time choices.

He then gave me a time he could stop by to pick up the legal documents he had requested. I reminded him that I am not interested in providing any documents to him until I receive the original title to my apartment. My kids would be happy to see their grandparents. Would they please stop by and see their grandchildren prior to their departure? They chose to not come and see my kids/their grandchildren before leaving.

By now over two months had passed since my parents had visited my husband's parents for the spring equinox and their arrival to the United States. Upon their departure from the United States, my husband's parents finally decided to repay the visit to my parents.

What was the purpose of this futile visit? *Talk sense into your daughter so she gives us the legal documents before we leave.*

They didn't like it when my husband had my back.
They didn't like it when my older sister had my back.
They didn't like it when my friends had my back.
They didn't like it when my parents had my back.
They didn't like it ever when I had my own back.

I'm thinking, seeing their grandchildren is not important but getting documents from me is? It wasn't that long ago, I got screwed because I handed over documents to them. Fool me once, shame on you. Fool me twice, shame on me. Why would I give you documents? Documents that make it easy for you to sell my apartment in Iran. The apartment that as you informed me doesn't even belong to me, per Iranian law.

Their loss for not spending the time they had been gifted with their own blood.
Their loss to give power more priority than their own grandchildren.
Their loss for not having personal accountability.

May there be realization that prioritizing money over family is a sin.
May there be realization that prioritizing money over family damages one's essence.
May there be realization that prioritizing money over family causes good people to have bad behavior.

May Peace and Love heal lost souls.
May Peace and Love heal all souls.
May Peace and Love heal our world.

Chapter Twelve
People Outreach

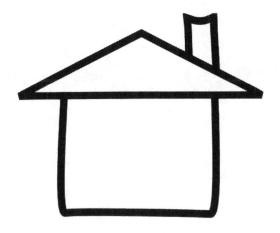

Isn't it easier to sit home in the world of Protection
Rather to stand outside in the world of Interaction

I didn't want to reply to people's outreach.
Because that would only confirm that he was gone.

I didn't want to do his laundry or get rid of his clothes.
Because it made it seem like he was still here.

I didn't want to believe he was gone.
Because it made life seem a bit more stable.

After all, I had been alone plenty of times in our marriage.
Our children were young and he traveled for business for
weeks on end. I held down the fort. Took care of everyone
and everything. This could be one of those times.

I would take those impossible days back if it meant he was
physically here with me.

I was so grateful when the hard days were behind us.
I would tell my husband how grateful I was.
I would tell God how grateful I was.

I felt like all my resilience in life had been rewarded. All my
patience and love had paid off. Now, I had the life I had
desired. I had a husband who was able to show his love. I had
a peaceful home and marriage.

For every high, there must be a low.
I had forgotten that part.
I had forgotten there must be a low.

In my low, I did my best to ignore messages.
In my low, I did my best to avoid seeing people.
In my low, I did my best to be present only for my children.

I just needed the time to myself, for myself.
And then, there comes those rare occasions when I respond.

5:45 a.m.
A text is received.

It is Fashion Friend.
Are you up?
I text back that I am.

She calls.
I had a dream about your husband.

He was wearing a white button down top.
His Tombstone picture that I chose has him wearing a white
button down top!

His hair was longer than his usual army cut.
I had always wanted him to have his hair just a little bit longer.
Still short, just not army style.

He was happy.
The setting is your home.
I knew he had been at home with me. This is why I sense love
in every aspect of my home. This is why I am happy staying
home.

He stood in your living room with me.
He told me how he enjoys parties and people
remembering him.
We rebuilt our home with parties in mind. I need to have
more friends over and get out of my rut.

He said we all should talk more often about him.
My kids don't talk about their dad. Maybe it is too painful.
Maybe everyone is busy with their own lives, except for me. I
keep him alive in my conversations with my children and
others. I feel like I'm climbing uphill trying to keep him in my
conversations. When he says we should talk more often about
him, I have just been given a new lift to carry on.

I was so excited to see your husband, I told him to wait
while I find your wife.
I looked outside the window and saw you sadly sitting
under a tree alone.

I started to come towards you and when you looked up, it wasn't you.
I did not recognize the face.
I stare out that window, from my contemplation seat, looking at that same tree with sadness.
I ran inside and there was a party in the house for your older daughter.
I found her and said, come with me. Your father is here.
She comes with me, however she cannot see her dad.
I ask your husband to give me some information so your older daughter knows her father is here.
Your husband says, tell her I like small tattoos.
Suddenly, your door opens and billions of balloons come from the sky into your home.
Heart shaped balloons, the size of my hand, three in a bunch.
One Red, One Pink, and One Lavender.

Then I woke up.

Does this mean anything to you?
Yes it does. Every detail does.

Does your older daughter want to get a tattoo?
No she doesn't. I had wanted to place a small tattoo on my leg. My husband was against it.

This means we have to get your tattoo, Fashion Friend proclaims.
I no longer desire that tattoo.

I am happy at home.
I want to stay home where I can feel my husband's energy.
I want to stay home where I can write.

When I'm out, I don't know how to respond to people asking me *How are you.* My older sister was having the same problem answering the question *How is your sister doing.*

We got to work and brainstormed on how my kids and I have been doing in order to have a prepared answer. We discovered that we are just managing and coping one day at time. So it was. On the rare occasions that someone would see me and ask me how I am, I had two standard answers to choose from. Today is a good day. I appreciate you asking. Or I'm managing and coping one day at a time.

Honestly, it is much easier to just stay home.

When I have gone out of the house it has been because of the persistence and love of family and friends.

Childhood Friend was going to a poetry reading at the Stanford Bookstore. The poetry reading was by one of her college friends. Childhood Friend came and picked me up so we could go together.

Childhood Friend went to the very fancy Menlo College in Atherton. I recalled her fancy college friends when I would visit her from my hick town.

We made it to the poetry reading.
The Carousel of Life.

The Poet brought tears to my eyes.
I was in the beautiful.
I was moved, touched, and inspired.

The Poet brought guilt to my heart.
The Life Growing In My Hair.

I was such an observer of life that I had paid no attention to the lice who invaded my home. Having had active kids in our American public school system and in theatre, lice and I were no strangers. Lice were friends that would stop by for short visits every so many years. Now that my guard was down and I was void of life, lice decided to overstay their welcome for months upon months.

I had had the experience of checking hundreds of other children's hair for lice while volunteering in my children's elementary school years before.

Now I was not even able to step up in my own life. Off and on, I tried to clear the lice by diligently combing through hair. I bagged beddings and other soft material. I vacuumed my mattress. I threw away hairbands and more. But then the lice would show up again. My heart felt the guilt of not being able to manage my lice situation. My older sister finally stepped in and had my home professionally lice cleaned the same day she had our hairs professionally cleared. Once again, she prevailed on my behalf by managing my life situation.

The Poet also brought curiosity to my mind.
I was in the expanding.
I was in the learning.

Then we saw Glamour Girl in the audience.
Glamour Girl had beautiful flipping hair in the 1980's.
She knew she was richer than and made sure you knew it too.

Childhood Friend suggested that we go over and say hello.
Before we knew it, Glamour Girl was saying hello to us.
Decades had passed. She still possessed the e$$ence of rich, youthful beauty.

I was surprised— she recalled Childhood Friend's Simple Friend.
Simple Friend would be me.
Childhood Friend asked her how life had been.
Glamour Girl shared how she is now married and living in Milan with her designer husband.

I blurted out how I love Spain.
Glamour Girl stared at me with disapproval.

Childhood Friend stepped in to correct me.

She is not living in Spain. She is living in Portugal.

Glamour Girl was taken aback. *No, it is not Portugal.*
Childhood Friend got confused that it was not Portugal.
You must be living in Brazil then.

Glamour Girl looked puzzled. She wasn't sure if we were
joking with her or if we are just dumb and dumber.

She corrected the two of us.
Milan is in Italy.

Oh, I knew that.

Childhood Friend, still astray, asked Glamour Girl about her
speaking Portuguese.
Glamour Girl corrected us again by letting us know she speaks
Italian not Portuguese.

The conversation ended.

We walked away realizing how silly we were.
How silly we looked.
How silly the whole interaction was.

We started to laugh.
We genuinely laughed.
We couldn't stop laughing.

Ok— deep inside, I was glad Childhood Friend took me out.

Still, I wished to spend most of my time at home where I feel
my husband's love in every corner. Loved it most when
friends would stop by.

From the very beginning, Pillar Friend was there for me. Even prior to my kids and I coming home, she was on Team Clean Up. She had bought new beddings and redone the trauma scene of my bedroom. Pillar Friend came by Wednesday mornings to check in on me at home, with groceries in hand. She would make me walk around the block with her. After a while, on Wednesday mornings, she would take me out so we could get groceries together. In time, on Wednesdays, she would stop by to make sure my refrigerator was filled with food for my kids and me.

The first time I went grocery shopping by myself was terrifying. I kept forgetting what was needed. I didn't have my usual list with me. I was floating in the space called a grocery store. I finally made it to the cashier where I was asked *How are you.* I started to cry. As loving as the cashier was, she only had a minute to push me through and get to the next person in line.

Pillar Friend later told me that she had searched the Internet on ideas for how to help a widowed friend, from where came the idea of handling groceries. There is a reason Pillar Friend is a Pillar. She put ideas into action.

My older sister had the ultimate "get out of your home" idea. Get out of town. Pillar Friend joined in. My older sister's husband's family was having a reunion in Croatia. His family is my honorary family. My older sister pulled the impossible. A trip to Europe for everyone. My mom, My older sister and her family, Me and my kids, My younger sister and her family, Pillar Friend and her family, My Helpful cousin and her son, and other friends who joined in!

In the simplest of moments, the greatest of grieving occur. Seated on that plane ride to Europe, my tears wouldn't stop. My husband loved to travel. My heavy heart was in pain.

Upon arrival and walking through passport control, memories of our first trip to Europe together consumed me. How he had a Schengen Travel Visa that was incorrectly dated for the day after our arrival. How we discovered this on the plane ride and had a lengthy discussion on what to do in order to manage our situation. We thought we'd split up. He can go first and if he is not allowed to enter, I can walk over to help.

We did split up. My husband passed through passport control in a breeze. I went up to the same Officer. I got stuck with question after question. I had so badly wanted to say that the person in front of me didn't even have a valid visa to enter your country, what are you doing questioning me?????

And so I was astounded later in that trip, standing together at the border of France when his passport didn't even get opened to be checked for that travel visa. My passport that didn't even require a visa got opened and checked.

Every moment of my current Europe trip was a trigger for memories. The time my husband and I were in Spain and hungrily walked into a restaurant. We were seated. It took forever to get a menu. So I asked for a Menu. We were booted out of that restaurant. The waiter kept repeating, *No Menu, No Menu.*

I couldn't believe we were kicked out of a restaurant for just asking to see a menu. Days later, we figured out because McDonald's had a "McMenu" option, some restaurants had a "Menu", which referred to a special deal. The proper word to use in Spain is *Carte* not *Menu.*

Memories were sweet to recall. What was most painful during this European trip was being in the homes of family and friends where my husband and I had been together. Now I realized, We would never be together again.

In all my years traveling, I had never had such an outpouring of love and care from both family and friends traveling with my kids and me, as well as from family and friends we were visiting.

Upon our return from Europe, my older cousin was visiting from Oregon.   His younger brother was my cousin whose cancer was too brutal and took him away on Valentines Day many a years ago.

My family went out to a Persian restaurant in town to celebrate my cousin's visit. I ran into two people who knew of me.

Certain Persian comments that have a sarcastic cultural undertone, necessitating one to defend oneself, always amuse me.

The first person I saw, in obvious wonder to see me says, in true Persian fashion, *You are out and about and looking happy.*

Couldn't he ask, *How are you*? I had canned answers for that.
Seriously, you are out and about and look happy?
How does a recent widower reply?
Not only am I out to a restaurant, I also chew gum, and watch movies.
Do I say, last time I saw you, eight months ago, it was my husband's funeral and I was in a state of shock? Now I have accepted my life and must carry on.
Do I explain that I'm not happy?
Just because I'm out and choosing to smile doesn't equate to my heart being happy. I am consciously choosing JOY.

Instead I replied, that it is kind of you to notice that today I am choosing joy. I'm pretty sure I just confused him.

The second person I ran into at the Persian restaurant asked the normal *How are you* (Yay, I had an answer) and then with heavy sarcastic undertone he dove into, *I heard you went to Europe.*

What does this mean?
Yes, I did go to Europe.
Am I not supposed to go?
Is it a sin to travel seven months after a loved one dies?

Why would someone say, *I heard you went to Europe.*
Should I have asked, from whom did you hear it?
What do you think of the fact that I was in Europe?

I just smiled at him and ignored the comment. Asked about his wife and kids instead.

I hadn't realized the extent to which I would be under the scrutiny of judgment.

Mind Note— Stay away from those I sense are judging me.
Mind Note2— Stay away from those I sense are gossiping.
Mind Note3— Stay at home. It is the most comfortable place to be and not face life.

My husband has two very smart cousins who got accepted to graduate school studying engineering straight from Iran. My husband and I made an effort to see them as much as possible. When my husband passed away, Cousin One came by often to check in on me. Once she stopped by my home as I laid lifeless on my couch. She made dinner for my girls and me. Cousin One tried to help me as much as she could. I am forever grateful for this generosity.

Cousin One invited my daughters to her town for a Society of Women Engineers program that her company had hosted. My girls loved how their minds opened to new possibilities. I loved that they got to hold on to their father's family even though my husband's brother and sister had not even called me once to see how we were. It felt important to me to keep any connection for my kids with their father's side of the family.

I was drinking tea one day and I texted Cousin One to let her know that I am sending her blessings for the delightful tea she had gifted me.

She gave me the news that Cousin Two, her sister, had a baby girl. I was elated for her. I love children and that is the one thing that truly brings me joy, new life.

I thought, I'm going down to Santa Barbara with my son to check out his new school— why not drive to Pasadena to see the newborn? It was a complicated weekend with juggling my girls, my son, and my sisters with their children. However, I was determined to make the visit happen because I knew it was what my husband would have done.

So I did.
I made the impossible possible.
I was happy doing it.
I was doing it in the name of my husband for the family he and I loved.

I made it to Pasadena from Santa Barbara for a short visit with the newborn. Upon my arrival, after my long trip, I sensed a bit of standoffishness from my husband's Uncle. Had I forgotten? His brother is my husband's father. I'm sure blood is thicker than water was the case here. Truly, love is thicker than blood. My husband's uncle's lovely wife sat next to me and we talked about life.

My life.
My broken life.

My broken heart.

How God gives me hope when I have had none.
How in wanting to be of service to others is where I find hope.

I talked about a woman I had recently met. She lost her husband two years ago. She is still a mess. Her home is full of clutter, like my mind is now. She lost her sister only two months after having lost her husband. An employee of her husband's company stole accounts and left to start a new competing company. She lost much needed income and did not have the energy to sue for what was rightfully hers. Her husband's family, the only family she has in the area, never came around and has basically abandoned her and her children. She has had many problems with her teenage kids. She has never gone to grief therapy and neither have her kids.

I talk about how I'm in therapy and so are my kids.
I talk about how we practice gratefulness.

The mother of Cousins is a truly down to earth woman of love. She shared how the loss of her brother still haunts her to this day, though a decade has passed. Just finding a piece of paper with his writing will trigger her. I understood. I fully understood this relevant experience.

The mother of Cousins made a comment that conflict is a norm of life, especially during weddings or funerals. How one should not be offended by other's comments. I realized she meant I should not be offended. I realized she had no clue about my interactions with my husband's family.

I made my comment to her. I truly hope those who get offended over other's comments find peace and love in their hearts.

I was about to leave but they had a spread for breakfast laid out on the kitchen counter. To be polite, I joined them.

By this time, my husband's Uncle had also warmed up.
A part of me knows that I am my husband.
My husband is with me in my heart.
And I know my husband is me in the eyes of others.
We were one.
Seeing me is seeing him.
Warming up to me is warming up to him.

As we were having breakfast, Cousin Two said *I heard you went to Europe.*

Is it possible this comment was lost in translation and I don't understand?

This is my hardest lesson in life to learn.
God knows I am working on it.

The lesson is others are not me.
They are themselves.

People don't think like I do.
People don't have the experiences I have had in life.
People do and say the best they know how.

People, Europe is not a big deal.

The implication, it seemed to me, was that somehow I am off having fun in Europe when my husband, her cousin, had passed away.

I live in awareness of when I am being judged.
I live in striving to not pass judgment.

Though there was not a need, I set the record straight with my husband's Cousin Two. I regressed to The Justifier in me.

We went to Germany to visit my Aunts.
They mourn the loss of my husband.
They wanted to see my kids and me to make sure we are okay.

They needed us there to process what had happened.

Did your husband, our cousin, know your Aunts?
YES. Of course. My husband and I had been together for 24 years. YES, when we visited my husband's and your older Uncle in London, we always stopped by Berlin to visit my Aunts. My Aunts came to the United States for our wedding. We visited them in all stages of our lives.

Without Children.
With one Child.
With two Children.
With three Children.
With three Kids.

You went to Italy too.
Really? I'm being told I went to Italy too?

My older daughter stayed on to visit Italy with her cousin. My sisters and I had visited Italy when we were in our teenage years. We felt it was important for our girls to have the same experience.

So you didn't visit Italy?
YES. I did visit Italy.
My older sister's husband had a family reunion in Croatia. We went to my older sister's husband's Italian cousin's home in Northern Italy and from there we drove to Croatia. YES, it is also my family reunion, because my older sister married her childhood friend. Our families are connected. I knew everyone at the reunion. Not only those coming from the United States; I am even friends with the Italians. Not only do I know the Italians, so did my husband. Why? Because my husband and I were One. We were together for 24 years.

If my husband's Uncle Herd cared to know, the Italians were also deeply saddened by my husband's loss and needed to see my kids and I to make sure we were okay. If they also cared to know, Italian family did more in the form of making sure my kids and I are okay than my own husband's birth family had ever done to date.

And I got tired. Why am I explaining myself for having gone on a trip to visit family and friends?

I got the why after I left and had time for reflection. Maybe, they have never been to Europe and for them going to Europe is a novelty. For me, it is the same as going to Ohio to visit with family and friends. I had traveled all over Europe as a child with my parents, as a teenager with my sisters, as a young adult with my friends, and as an adult with my husband yet later with our children.

For me, novelty will be when I go Tanzania. Or when I visit Iceland. Maybe I would ask with fascination about Safari experiences. Or would want to hear the wonder of the Nordic Lava Fields.

Would I ever use an undertone to say, I heard you went to Iceland. NO.
I would say, with a loving smile, I'm so excited for you. Is it true you went to Iceland?
I would ask in wonderment, How was Iceland?
I would say with curiosity, Tell me about Iceland. I would love to go one day.

I wanted to leave at that moment and was about to say goodbye to my husband's Uncle Herd, when Cousin One says that my husband's sister is stopping by. She wanted me to know in the event I wanted to leave.

Well, I had wanted to leave. Not because my husband's sister was now coming. Because I felt drained having to explain I had been to Europe. Now that Cousin One said what she said, it looked like I wanted to leave because my husband's sister is coming. What does that matter anyway?

I leave. I said goodbye and left.

At this point, I don't care what anything seems like to others.
At this point, I don't care to explain myself to people.
At this point, I don't care to be around those I sense are judging me.

I leave and think to myself, I am glad I visited Cousin Two. It was very kind of me.
I leave and think to myself, I did it for the love of my husband and his honor.
I leave and think to myself, she is a young mother who probably lacked sleep.

I know in my heart people are doing the best they know how.
I know in my heart people are doing the best they are able.

My work in progress is to live in awareness of being judged without *Judgement*.

It is at this time that I do The Boat Exercise.
Life is a river.
We are riding life on board our boat. Who are the people on board with us? My husband fell out on December 16th, 2016. With him gone, some others have decided to jump off as well.

I do not have the need to hold on to people and make them stay.
I do not feel rejected if they decide to leave.

I have accepted the leaving.
I welcome the freedom of choice to leave.

Leaving makes room for others who wholeheartedly want to hop on board my boat.

There are also many wholehearted people I want to have on my boat. There is the matter of space on each other's boats. I'm most grateful for moments of love shared with wholehearted people not on board.

Chapter Thirteen
Messenger

A labyrinth is a labyrinth.
It openly flows from start to finish.

A maze is a maze.
It has blocks from start to finish.

I keep getting flat tires this year.
Different vehicles, different flat tires.
Is it an illustration of my airless life?

In my younger days it would have been nothing for me to change tires, the oil in my car, or windshield wipers. In my older days, I have entirely stopped. I get stomped doing things that were second nature decades before.

About a month into my husband's passing, I felt like my world was swirling around me. I needed to get control. I grabbed one swirling item out of the air in an effort to bring order. The cars. I started to check the vitals of our cars. Oil levels, Brake fluid levels, Coolant levels, Tire PSI, and anything else I could think of.

One evening when I walked into our garage to grab paper towels, I smelled a strange smell. I jumped inside our home and called 911. I made my reluctant kids leave go outside. I thought we had a gas leakage. The fire trucks came just as they had on our dreadful morning. The Hazards Material Team suited up and entered our garage. We were asked to leave the premises. Our neighbors had worried that something had happened to me this time and were relieved to see all of us safe.

We were called back into our home and asked if we had changed the oil our car. My kids glared at me. I started apologizing to the Fire Fighters. I'm so sorry to drag you out here for a self-created false alarm. The Fire Fighters reassured me that I was right to call them. I should call again and anytime in doubt. They assured me that there is no reason for an apology.

I realized that I had not fully closed the oil cap on my car. The oil had leaked and caused the smoke and the smell.

My kids made it clear to me that while living in hick town centuries ago where I had to take care of things myself, we now lived in a metropolitan area with lots of resources. *Don't try to do things yourself again.*

I tried to explain to them that my soul mate was gone. I needed to do something. I can't just sit around. It wasn't about outsourcing to change my car oil. It was about getting control of a life that feels so out of control.

Many months later, I was with my dad. We experienced one of my many flat tires in that year. I pulled over.

I called AAA roadside assistance.
As with everything that had gone wrong, AAA joined that party.

A couple of months prior when I was in the AAA office taking care of changing the car titles to my name, the clerk initiated the removal of my husband from the roadside assistance package. The following week, a new roadside assistance card came in the mail in my husband's name. I figured the clerk had made a mistake of deleting me instead of my husband. And then, one more item got added to my to-do list. Go to AAA and get my own roadside assistance card back and cancel my husbands.

Now I had a flat tire and I was on the phone with AAA who said I was not the cardholder. Well that is because you had made the mistake. The cardholder is my deceased husband.

God has had my back. An angel in the form of a human stopped on the side of the road to help me put that spare tire on. I couldn't hold back my tears of gratefulness. I was able to take my 86-year-old dad back home after his day of adventure. I immediately went to the tire shop to see if my flat tire was fixable. They told me the wait would be 4 hours.

I walked out and thought, who can I call that could pick me up? I don't have my husband to call. I start to cry.

In that moment, my cell phone rang. It was Messenger. Messenger and his wife were friends of ours when we had toddlers and babies. As life happens, we didn't maintain our friendship. I really liked his wife. She wasn't fan enough of my spaciness combined with stark honesty. My husband wasn't fan enough of Messenger's ramblings.

I thought, he is calling, as many caring people have, to see how I'm holding up. Messenger must have caught my tears when I said hello. After the greetings, I poured out how difficult life had become even in the everyday simplicity of it.

Messenger said he wants to stop by and meet me to talk about finances. I'm thinking what? Talk about what finances?

I suggest that I have plenty of time, 4 hours, now to talk. He says he prefers to do it in person. He has known others who had lost spouses. He wished he would have talked to them about this important financial matter. Maybe he could have had a positive impact on their now financially dire situations. I'm thinking he wants to sell me a multi-level-marketing product that has been making money for him.

I can't wrap my head around selling products in this time of my life. I can't even wrap my head around expanding my own business.

As kindhearted as I am, I said that I'd meet with him.

My son picks me up from the tire shop and I inform him of the call. I beg my son to be home when Messenger wants to stops by so I'm not alone. We talked about how we will politely listen to Messenger's presentation, learn something new, and then stand strong in our assertion that we are not in a capacity now to sign on to a new business venture.

The following week he stops by. He walks in with flowers. He is in awe of our newly built home. When our kids were young, his family had also wanted to remodel. Looking back at the process of building our home, I realize it was an emotionally difficult step to take. I was sensitive to his position of not yet having remodeled and downplayed our rebuild.

I offered him some tea and brought him his requested water. He started talking about this and that. I kept trying to bring him back to focus on his purpose for the visit. So what kind of work are you doing now? How had life been for you since your lay off?

Finally, my no nonsense son asked *Why are you here*?

Messenger told us that he had been in Iran for a visit. He had the opportunity to visit my husband's father. He has come to give us a message.

My God, he is not here for me to join an MLM company? How can I be so naïve? Of course, I get it now. How did we meet all those years ago? Messengers father and my husband's father are friends in Iran.

I take a deep breath.
He tells me I should pick up the phone and call my husband's sister and brother.

I want to say, are you kidding me?

I want to say, my husband's sister who accuses my husband of stealing money from his own family? Who accuses me of wanting to steal my own kids' money?

I want to say, my husband's brother who gladly accepted back his gift money of $1,000? My husband's brother who wanted to extort his parents' gift money from me?

Instead, I let him know that my husband has passed for eight months now. Neither his sister nor brother had called me in these months to see how I am holding up.
How my kids are holding up.
How they can be of support to us.
How they can see my kids and spend time with them.

What exactly would you like me to call and say to them?

Messenger then suggests that I am keeping my kids away from my husband's family. I made it clear that my kids were not babies and toddlers that "Evil me" has locked up in my home, not allowed to be seen.

Realizing he wouldn't get anywhere with me, he shifted gears.

Next, he told my son how there is millions of dollars at stake here. *Don't be stupid. Pick up the phone and call your rich grandfather if you don't want everything to go to your Aunt and Uncle after he dies.*

I cannot believe the message. My son should call because there are millions of dollars at stake? Is he admitting that they have strings attached to have their own grandchildren receive monetary wealth?

My son replied.
> *If my grandfather wants to talk to me, he can call me. Isn't it inefficient to send you from Iran to come to our home and ask me to call him?*
>
> *My mother has been disrespected with abusive behavior. I will not have a relationship with those who disrespect her. If they truly care about us, it is up to them to make it right.*

Realizing he can't get anywhere with my son, he redirected with me. *I know your mother-in-law can seem harsh. Everyone has mother-in-law problems. Do you really want to ruin the financial future of your kids because of her?*

I inform him that I don't have a problem with my husband's mother.
I inform him that I don't have any problems with my husband's mother.

She never liked me.
She has never hid it from me.

Puzzlingly, I respect her truth on this matter.
Wholeheartedly, I respect her attempt at a remorse offered.

I simply have a problem with conniving people.

He was confused.
      Are you going to pick up the phone and call your in-laws?

No, I am not calling.
If your wife were abused, would you make her pick up the phone and call her abuser?

These people believe they can step all over me with no consequences.
These people believe maintaining power is more important than love.
These people believe monetary wealth is more important than family.

Wealth is important, I agree.
But don't you see that kindness is a far more valuable currency than money?
Don't you see that our souls get weary under the burden of money?

And may I add that you have made things worse. Now if ever my son wants to call his grandparents, you have planted the seed in his mind that my son calling equates to being a beggar of their money.

Messenger claimed that they want to see my kids. I shared that despite their heinous behavior, my door has always been open to my husband's parents. I just don't recall anyone asking me to see my kids and me rejecting the idea.

Messenger then went on to say that they would like to financially help us but I'm not allowing them.

Really? In our last conversation on that topic, I owed them money. I explained one either does something or doesn't. Wanting to do something is just noise. If they truly want to help, they have our address and they can put a check in the mail. No one is stopping them but themselves.

Messenger had no limits. He went on to ask how I can afford to live in this nice home. How much longer before I fail and can't pay my mortgage.

Is this part of the message? The Herd is waiting for me to fail so I go begging them for money?

I reinforce that I am capable of handling of my finances. I have God, and my generous parents behind me.

I nicely ended the ugly visit saying that I know he has a big heart and is only a Messenger. I would be more than happy to look at their house plans and give feedback to him based on my experience. I will always remember him for the Saturday morning that he stopped by my house to fix my kitchen sink faucet after a dinner party the night before when he noticed my kitchen faucet wasn't working well.

He left.

Naive me spent several hours reviewing his house plans that he had emailed me sending suggestions, and sharing lessons learned by me. Plus, giving him hope to plunge forward knowing that the money and resources will show themselves once he shows up to do the work.

Then I found out that he ignored all that was exchanged the day of his visit. I found out, once again, how smart my husband truly was for not being a fan of his.

He texted my son saying, *Call your Uncle.*
My no nonsense son texted back, *Do not interfere in my life.*

He texted my son again saying, *Come to dinner at our house.*
My son texted back, *I will not. Stop contacting me.*

He then texted me to invite my kids and I for dinner. I said NO. I had known he crossed the line with my son. I had known he only called me because he didn't get anywhere with my son.

His wonderful wife texted me to have dinner with them. At this point, the answer remained a friendly no.

I am growing thicker and thicker skin by the day. Kind hearted people-pleasing me, who never wants to hurt a soul, can now more easily say no to people. If before, I danced around the space where Souls not knowing their limits invaded mine, I now know to say no.

You shall not invade my space.
You shall not prevail.

Within a week of this, my husband's brother sent a text to my kids with a picture of his son and daughter. The message read, *We miss you.*

My kids approached me with this text so we can discuss it as a family. I took turns asking each of them, what do you think of this text? How, if anyway, do you wish to reply?

Each of them went around and shared their thoughts. My younger daughter also asked *how would you reply if our Uncle and Aunt call to see us and are not remorseful for their past actions.*

In my reply, I set a new boundary for this non-existent relationship.

I clarified if they call me to see you my answer is a reluctant yes. As I have maintained, my moral compass will not allow me to keep you away from your dad's family. The only change we have made thus far is that I am no longer initiating interaction with them.

If they call without remorse, we can meet at a park for a set period of time and they can see you under my supervision.

If they call and are truly remorseful, we can meet in our home and for Birthdays, Weddings, and Graduations. All they wanted anyway was to see you for your milestones. They will never be welcomed back into my everyday life, which for now includes my underage daughters.

My kids and I had a laugh reminiscing about their younger days. Would saying I'm sorry suffice as remorse? I would have to reply as I did when my kids were young. I'm sorry means you will do something different next time. What will you do differently?

My kids all concurred that the right move for their Aunt and Uncle was to stop playing games by sending texts excluding their mother on purpose.

We miss you with a picture of our cousins. What does that mean anyway? We miss you. If dad's family truly cares and misses us, they would pick up the phone, call our mother, and request a time to see us.

I was in awe of my self-reliant kids.
I was in awe of my mother-loving kids.
I was in awe of my no-nonsense kids.

I don't believe any of them replied to that mind game of a text.

Then came my own Messenger. Old Man is my Hostess cousin's husband's father. Old Man is in his late 80's and wants there to be peace as older wiser people want to experience in our world. He approached me to share what a great man my husband's father is. I agreed with him. He goes on to tell me that they had had a long conversation at my husband's memorial.

He told me how grandchildren are precious and he can't live without his. *Are you making your grandchildren available to their grandparents?* I tell him, yes I have made my kids available. I am pro my kids having a HEALTHY relationship with their father's family.

Certain events have put a damper on our relationship. At this point, if my husband's parents truly care and want to be with their grandchildren, it is their responsibility to contact us. I am no longer interested in chasing after them, begging them to spend time with my kids. My heart had broken for my husband when he did. It is too painful for my emotional capacity to do the same now.

Do you have a clear conscience regarding this matter? Yes, I do. I know, feel, and sense it in my heart. I have a clear conscience. I live in the truth.

Several weeks later, Old Man called me. *I called your husband's father in Iran. I asked him if he wants a relationship with his grandchildren and good news he said he would consult with his wife.*

I was thinking seriously, you asked him and instead of a solid "YES of course" I want a relationship with my grandchildren he replied he has to consult with his wife?

Sure, if you think this is good news Old Man, I'll say that it is great news. Then he went on to inform me that they are under the impression that I will call the police if they call my home.

What do I say?
How does one reply to nonsense?
Last I checked, calling someone is not against the law.

I said this is exactly why they are not in my life. I can't handle their lies and unfounded attacks.

Old Man, you have been around, they eat me for breakfast.

Old Man told me the story of compassion in his life. When an employee had made a mistake and then lied to cover it. Instead of firing the employee, Old Man showed compassion and mercy.

Old Man, are you asking me to show mercy? They made a mistake and now are covering it with lies?

I'm the most merciful person I know. I forgive and give second chances and yet forgive again too often in my life. What I'm dealing with here are spoiled children grown up to be spoiled adults that have no regard for the natural consequences of the choices they have made.

It sounds like your employment situation was a one-time occurrence. It sounds like you didn't have to face this person in your personal life. I have a lifetime of hurt occurrences with the Herd. I believe if the Herd is given an opening, they will not hesitate to intrude negatively in my personal life.

Old Man told me he needs to call them again to see what my husband's mother would say about having a relationship with their grandchildren.

I told Old Man if it is a matter of importance to them, they will call you and let you know. Live and Let Live. He insisted he gave his word that he would call back and so he must.

Old Man called me again.
> *Great News. If you just pick up the phone and call them, they are willing to call your older daughter to wish her a Happy Birthday.*

Old Man, I will not call. Whether or not they call their granddaughter for her birthday should have nothing to do with me.

On a side note, I did not call. They called their granddaughter on her birthday and spoke to her. One of two times they called from Iran in that year. The second phone call was to blame me for my son not returning their phone call.

Old Man went on to explain.
> *So they made mistakes. So they are sharks and you can't swim with them in the same waters. It's not like they killed anyone. How can you say you are compassionate and a person of God, yet not call your husband's parents? Imagine how your husband would feel about this?*

How my deceased husband feels about my not calling his abusive parents?

Could it be I'm young and naïve?
Could it be that wisdom has no age?
Could it be that relevant experience makes compassion?

Old Man, have you ever been raped?
I shock him with my question.

I have.
I have been raped.
My spirit has been raped.

In a time of great vulnerability in my life, predators you call
sharks attacked, injured, and insulted my husband and my
being.

I realize that love prevails.
I realize on the other side of right and wrong there is existence.
I realize that my heart wants them to do what I would do.
Apologize.
I realize that my soul wants them to be what I am.
Considerate.

You are asking me to give more power to predators.
You are asking me to call them because they demand it.

Or wait. Are you asking me to give love to those who do not
warrant it?
Can't I give that love spiritually without the action of calling?

Old Man.
I have to honor my being.
I have to honor my rawness.
I have to honor my wish that I do not wish to call them.
I have to honor my intelligence that I do not have a reason to
call them.
I have to honor my purity that I only want to be left in peace
from them.

I am compassionate.

I wish them heart in their lives.
I wish them light in their lies.
I send loving energy for their healing.

Being compassionate and merciful does not mean that I
should allow them back into my life.
Being compassionate and merciful does not mean that I give in
to their demands and call them.

Being compassionate to me means knowing that what has
happened has happened. Accepting it as I have.

Knowing that there is probably a higher purpose in all of this
that I cannot yet grasp.
Knowing that their souls have a purpose as mine does.
Knowing that I'm grateful they have made me an even
stronger person.

Maybe we all agreed to this arrangement prior to our births.
Maybe my standing strong is for them to learn their learning.
Maybe this is my karma from something I had done to them in
a previous life.

Could it be that this is exactly how life was supposed to
happen?
Every moment of every minute of every day is our collective
destiny.

I am open for them to find remorse.
I am open for them to find peace.
I am open for them to find their grandchildren.

I am making a choice to share my truth.

This choice within the structure of my destiny, I made to heal
my being. As a result, I believe that my choice will also heal
their beings.

I am making a choice to not contact them.

This choice within the structure of my destiny, I made to advance my soul. As a result, I believe that my choice will also advance their souls.

Because we are all seeds of the same fruit.
Because we are all humans of the same family.
Because we are all souls of the same universe.

I am Compassion.
I am Courage.
I am Conscience.

We are Compassion.
We are Courage.
We are Conscience.

God is Compassion.
God is Courage.
God is Conscience.

God is Reason.
God is Love.
I am Love.
God is I.

Chapter Fourteen
My Relationship

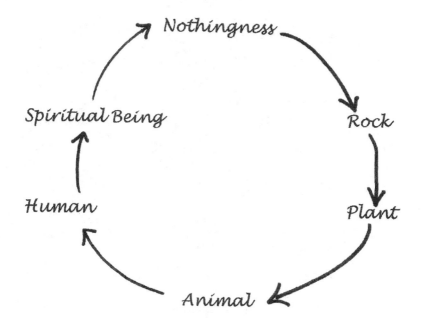

As I am standing in the grocery line, I hear the robotic clerk ask the person in front me, *How are you?* The clerk is not really looking for an answer from this loaded question. The man in line suddenly can't hold back his tears. The clerk stays silent waiting for the transaction to complete and the customer to walk away. I'm up next and the clerk asks me, How are you. I just smile to say that today is a good day. I appreciate your asking.

I have relevant experience, so I recognize the pain.
My sensitive radars are on full force.

I'm sitting at the tire shop waiting for my car and I notice the lady next to me is distraught.
I ask her how she is holding up.
Shocked, she asks, *Is it so easy to tell from my face?*
I ask, would you like to share your load with me?
She shares her heaviness.
In return I share my heaviness.
As we depart, strangers realize how we carry one another.

All of life is an exchange of energy.

Sun gives plant energy so plant can sustain.
Plant gives me energy so I can sustain.

I give to you my positive energy. It leaves me with your negative energy.
You give to me your positive energy. It leaves you with my negative energy.

People only exchange negative and positive energies amongst themselves.
To protect our fellow humans, it is best for us to safely give water and nature our deep negativity to be replenished with positivity.

Drinking water.
Taking showers.

Going for a hike in nature.
Going for a walk down the street.
Focusing on trees and flowers.

Since this knowing, it had been a practice of mine to be
cognizant of my state of energy when interacting with others.

I was aware of the negativity I was carrying with me after my
husband's passing.
I was aware that fear overcame me as a result of the sudden
shake in my life.
I was aware of the depression that consumed me as a result of
my state of affairs.

There was still so much swirling in the air.
There was still so much I had no idea about.
There was still so much confusion and chaos.

My older sister had a plan.
Accomplish one item per week.
Celebrate your one item accomplished.

My older sister helped me make an initial list.
My older sister, Pillar Friend, and Fashion Friend's husband
would rally around me and take me out to make errands
happen.

Go to AAA to change the title of the cars.
Go to Banks to figure out and consolidate accounts.
Go to Cemetery and figure out what is needed for a tombstone.

One of my husband's Stanford friends stepped up and helped
with my husband's retirement plans. He was there to help
navigate the complicated correct move to make. The correct
move, for me, was to transfer my husband's retirement funds
into an inherited account.

One of my husband's childhood friends from Tennessee, whom I didn't even know well prior to my husband's passing, called me every week to check in on me. He got straight to business.

How will you survive financially?

I really wasn't sure how I could survive without my husband who was the main breadwinner.

Tennessee Friend would give me tasks and then call to check on how I had proceeded.

Tennessee Friend told me about Social Security.
    Call the office and make an appointment to go in.
I did.
They gave me an appointment for 3 months later.

It was the best call and visit I ever made.
It was Survivors Benefits.
It was money on the table that helped with our financial survival that I may have left behind otherwise.

The love of people around me powered me.

I knew I was not on my own.
I knew I couldn't do it on my own.
I knew I didn't have to do it on my own.

I started to immerse into our finances. I was so proud of myself. I came up with a strategic way to file both inside the file cabinet and on the computer that matched.

Home Organization:
    Critical Records
        Identity Documents
        Insurance Policies
        Taxes
        Titles and Deeds
        Trusts
        Vital Documents (Vital Documents are all those passwords and logins!)

    Records
        Home
        Medical (Doctor Visit summaries)
        Memories (Photos, Children School Projects, etc.)
        Receipts and Warranties
        Family Wellness (Time management, Exercise, Grief, etc.)

    Assets
        Retirement Accounts
        Brokerage Accounts
        Educational Accounts
        Bank Accounts
        Airline Mileage
        Social Security
        Investment Projects
        Business

    Liabilities
        Home Maintenance Expenses
        Medical Expenses
        Auto Expenses
        Credit Cards
        Mortgage

Creating this system gave me a sense of stability in a mind and world of clutter. I now had a structure within which to start placing everything around me in.

In the swirling world of disorder, I was reaching for order.

Order is divinity.
Order is peace.
Order is sanity.

Was order easy to achieve?
NO— so much that had no end or beginning.

I am learning to be kind to myself.
I am accepting where I am.
I am realizing, no matter what, I am Grateful.
I am remembering, no matter what, I am LOVE.

No. Matter. What.

My eating habits had taken a turn for the worse.
My mind knew it was more important than ever before in my
life to eat healthy so my brain can function and I can heal.

Initially, I had completely lost my appetite and couldn't eat
anything. Causing a sudden unhealthy weight loss.

As several months passed, I had completely gained an appetite
and would eat everything in sight. Stress eating. Causing a
gradual unhealthy weight gain.

My husband used to joke that he loves seafood.
Whatever foods he sees, he eats!

The overwhelming feeling of anxiety, trauma, and pressure
had me in a state of disarray. I skipped meals. I would eat
snacks. Though full with snacks, sometimes I'd have meals as
well. My level of consumption was high. My level of
nutritional intake was low.

I heard all the stories of how when one spouse passes, the
other gets sick. Real sick. I knew the basis of all disease is
inflammation. I got liver inflammation.

I broke down crying in the medical exam room. I was then offered antidepressant pills. How can I push through the pain of my grief if I'm sedated? How will my compromised liver survive the load of pills? I rejected the doctor's suggestion. No pill can save me. Only I can save myself.

I had to clean up my act now.
I had to go Gluten free.
I had to go Carb free.
I had to go Sugar free.
I had to eat meals regularly during the day.
I had to watch my food intake.
I had to have a set water intake.

I had to for the sake of my kids. I am all they have left in this world. I have to take care of myself so I can be there for them.

I have to.
I have to.
I have to.

Why is I have to so hard to do?

As a young child I was mute and starved.
This was true in the eyes of others.

People would tell me, I have to eat some meat and protein.
I would only stare back at them, without a word.

My paternal grandmother would tell me many stories. My birth family went back to Iran for a visit after my mom's mother had passed away. One of my paternal grandmother's children convinced my father to leave my mother.

Per Iranian law, we the kids, were taken from our mother. In this time period, my mom would watch us from the outside of the home where we were kept to make sure we were okay. We were not okay. It was in this time period that I was sexually abused. My siblings and I each recall this period as a time of despair in our lives for our own experiences. Though some adults believe that children do not understand or will not remember, this is not so. Children understand more and comprehend more than most adults.

My paternal grandmother would tell me stories of her shame carried for her child's actions. How she felt as a mother she had failed. How she tried to be a voice of sense and reason to no avail. I would tell her, yes you did to some avail because my father finally got his senses back and snapped out of the spell of his sibling. My father decided to flee the country that does not have women's rights with his wife and kids once again.

Is it the fear-based environment of Iran that promotes such savage behavior?
Is it the fear-based environment of the USA that promotes such savage behavior?
Is it the fear-based environment of the world that promotes such savage behavior?

My paternal grandmother had many a hardship of her own having lost her parents as a child. She was married off to her paternal cousin at the young age of fourteen. She had to work as a slave would for her mother-in-law. Finally, when her life was about to have order, she became a widow at a young age. She shared how she was an only parent of six, without a breadwinner. She lost social standing. She became a woman of God to survive.

She knew that repentance is an act of self.
She knew that evolution is the goal of humanity.
She knew that destiny must be embraced.

253

As a teenager, I had many a discussions with my paternal grandmother. I believed that our life is in our control. It is the decisions that we make that determine our destiny. She would tell me that our destiny is written in the stars.

This subject of destiny or choice haunted my being until I realized it had to be both. How? In learning how there is always a win-win situation, I was freed from my destiny or choice dilemma. We are destined for an experience and, within the structure of this destiny, we have choices that we make.

I would make a point to let my paternal grandmother know that modern day prophets are all men. It would be an honor for me to help her start a religion where she can become a woman prophet. She would be a heroine. How I made her laugh.

When my mother was finally reunited with her children, I was a young child who had become catatonic.
I never wanted to leave my mother's side.
I refused to be left alone.

When my mother would leave me at home to run errands, she would come back to a home where I had broken her favorite vase. She would come back to a home where I had ripped apart her favorite plant. She would come back to a home where I had made a mess of her most organized closet.

My parents were no longer allowed to travel alone. They would leave my siblings behind to go traveling together. But I would not be left behind. I would go everywhere with them.

Going to school was an ordeal. I refused to go to school. By first grade, I sat crying for hours refusing to walk into the school and then classroom. It took months of care from loving adults working at the school to ease me into going into the classroom.

I had become mute.
There was no need for words in my life.
I lived in silence.

I would talk very little.
I would eat very little.
Mostly plants.

I became an open portal.
I knew the grace of God had always protected me in the face of
Evil.
I sensed Godly spirits connecting to me.

As a child, I had become afraid of myself.
I discovered I could see the past and future.

I would think of something or see it in my mind.
I would see the same something happen in life outside of my
mind.
I would be confused. I did not understand.
I would wish for the visions to stop.

It was as simple as envisioning a car on fire.
And then driving by and seeing a car actually be on fire.

It was as harsh as envisioning everyone wearing black.
And then understanding that there had been a death in the
family.

It was as clear as envisioning specific visitors by our front
door.
And those exact people being at our front door.

I saw the spectrum of people.
I saw the energy of people.
I saw the destiny of people.

First there was nothingness.
Then came Rock.

From which came Plant.
From which came Animal.
From which came Human.
To which goes Spiritual Being.
To which goes nothingness.

That is the spectrum of humans.
When we become silent as a Rock we are able to propel to
Spiritual Being in the circle of life back to nothingness.

As we are all unfolding towards becoming Spiritual Beings,
there are those of us who are still animalistic in nature and
others who have achieved blessedness. There are days I can be
Animalistic and Blessed in one.

Animals have had to be fear-based for survival. Their
antennas need to be up to know when predators approach.
They need to become predators to survive.

Animals have never had the luxury of living in gratefulness. It
is a foreign concept brought about by blossomed humans who
have had the fortune of trusting life. As more and more
humans trust life and can live in gratefulness, less and less
humans will live in animalistic fear, thrusting our shift to the
next level of our human evolution.

I was a loner most of my young life.
I had my Childhood Friend.
I had my sisters.

I finally learned to stop seeing. Sometimes.
I finally learned to start living. Sometimes.
I was always aware that I lived and saw differently.

Now— if only now I can go back to eating just raw plants.
Now— if only now I can go back to Silence.

It is never about going back.
It is only about moving forward to reach the before.

It is about my learning.
It is about knowing that I must live LOVE to help move the human race forward.

How do I live LOVE?
I do call my husband's mother for my husband's 50th Birthday to acknowledge that she gave him life.

How do I live LOVE?
I do stop and notice people around me who need to unload their heaviness. As friends have shown me LOVE by taking my heaviness.

How do I live LOVE?
I do share my truth to give hope to all disheartened humans who have faced trauma of death, trauma of predatory behavior, or just trauma of our collective lives lived.

Chapter Fifteen
End of a Year

My younger sister was shopping at a grocery store as she walked down one aisle and found herself in front of Favorite Daughter-in-law. Favorite Daughter-in-law turned her face to the side, dissing my younger sister. My younger sister was caught off guard. Then Favorite Daughter-in-law's son smiled a big happy smile upon seeing my younger sister. My younger sister could not resist the child. She walked up to hug the boy and by default said hello to the dissing Favorite Daughter-in-law.

My younger sister called me in disbelief. Since the "issue" is with the Herd and me, my younger sister did not understand the reason she had been dissed by Favorite Daughter-in-law.

This brought a very important question to the forefront. What if anyone from my Tribe ran into any one from the Herd? Do we say hello? Do we wait for them to say hello first? And if they do, then do we reply to their hello?

I told my younger sister, I was already clear in my conviction. If I am to run into the Herd in the street, I will only reply to a hello from them. I will not speak first until the day they realize their offenses. Since almost a year has gone by, I can believe it will never happen. I am also starting to see more clearly with the separation and passing of time. I don't want their toxicity in my life again.

We were into November and December. These were the toughest months of the year for me. I had not realized how difficult it would be.

It was my husband's 50th birthday and without him. I had thought I would celebrate for him. I will have a party with his friends honoring his soul.

I did not.
I could not.
I did not have the bandwidth.

I had thought to myself I would get a massage or a manicure and pedicure. I could ironically use one of the many gift certificates my husband had gifted me.

I did not.
I could not.
I did not have the bandwidth.

I thought to myself my daughters and I could go out to dinner as the five us traditionally did for birthdays.

We did not.
We could not.
We did not have the bandwidth.

Instead, I was disheartened in bed all day. I did call and leave a message for my husband's mother, acknowledging she gave birth to my husband 50 years ago and how I was grateful to have had him in my life.

My older sister came to the rescue. She drove the girls and me down to Santa Barbara so my son could be included. We all went out to Mexican Food (my husband's favorite) to celebrate his soul.

Over and over again, I'm beside myself for the positive actions and affection towards me from family and friends. Over and over again, I'm beside myself with how family and friends lift my kids and I up with love. Over and over again, I'm beside myself for all the goodness in our world.

I know I'm blessed. All these fantastic unbelievable blessings are occurring around me. I know it was my husband from above who made it possible for me to secure a required loan. I know it was my husband from above who made it possible for me to write as I have. I know it is my husband hovering over my kids and me to ensure we can continue to live a life of goodness.

It is my birthday in the same month of November. I woke up and my husband wasn't there to bring me flowers and breakfast in bed as he did every year. I didn't feel like doing anything but crying.

In my mind, I'm grateful for everything and everyone around me.
In my heart, I'm in pain.

This deep pain has manifested itself into my physical body. I ache. My head aches. My neck aches. My entire upper and lower back aches. My hips and knees ache. I'm in so much pain I cannot walk straight. My son surprises me and comes home the day of my birthday. I am in awe of his love. He is there as a force, reminding me that we are strong and we will continue to live. My kids and I go out to our traditional family birthday dinner. My kids and I wish my husband could physically be with us.

Thanksgiving approaches. I have had an entire year of giving thanks for the love around me. I am once again reminded of my husband being grateful for his wife, for his children, and for all the Bay Area sports teams. We continue with tradition. We go to my younger sister's home and celebrate. We have a remembrance and a moment of silence for my husband. We purposefully choose joy. We laugh. We eat. We drink. We are merry. I'm in pain. I couldn't walk straight because of my pain.

I just couldn't believe it was already December. How can one year pass so easily? Was it so easily? It was a painful year. December 2nd was our anniversary. The second of every month this year I had recalled how we would have celebrated had he been here. December 2nd was especially hard for me. My older sister knew and had an entire evening planned of going to the theatre and dinner with friends who would keep me occupied. We all laughed with our good memories of my husband. I forgot my physical pain that night. I became young with my memories.

As December continues, I cannot. I'm in massive physical pain. I cry at nights and cannot fall asleep. I realize I have gained over 20 pounds this year. Is it my extra weight that has broken my body? Is it my heavy heart that has broken my body? Why, How, and What has done this?

I have sought Quantum Healing, Reiki, Feldenkrais, Acupuncture, Cupping, Chiropractic, Ultrasound Therapy, Massages, and Herbs. I have even succumbed to taking muscle relaxants and painkillers to no avail. The pain in my head, neck, back, hips, and knees agonizing.

I pled with God in the midst of my sleepless nights. Please forgive me any sins I may have unconsciously committed. Please take away my pain. I cannot bear it any longer. Allah Almighty, what do you need from me? I am forever your servant. Show me the path I need to be on. How much tolerance do you need me to have in this lifetime? I do not know if I am capable of what is required of me. Please Jesus, I can no longer bear this. I would rather die than to live with this pain.

I know it in my heart. God loves me. God has a plan for me. God not responding to my cries of help is part of this bigger plan for the greater good.

In the week leading to my husband's date of death, I time travel to our previous year. I am present in our past.

When we dutifully dropped off our older daughter to her friend's birthday party.
When we happily bought new goalkeeper gloves to surprise our younger daughter.
When we wanted to see how my son's college essays were coming along.
When my husband and I had fun shopping together.
When I made him buy a suit and tie to match our son.

When I got mad at him because I had told him to buy eggs and he came home forgetting the eggs. When I apologized for making a big deal about the eggs.

When I kissed him.

When we made love, he thanked me and I was in awe of his gratefulness.

When we went to the bank together to get my jewelry out of our safety deposit box.

When my older daughter curiously and spontaneously asked her dad how would she know vital information such as bank safety deposit boxes if she no longer had her parents.

When he wanted to give me a break and he made dinner for us.

When I was nervous the entire day before.

My mind thinking it was because we were traveling.

My heart knowing it was not because we were traveling.

When I rudely told my younger sister I don't want to be with her. I needed to go home and be with my husband, after she generously had treated me to a manicure and pedicure to calm my noticeable nerves.

When he spoke on the phone for a long time with his mother.

When I kissed my husband good night and said I love you before going to bed.

When I woke up to make sure he had finished paperwork and was in bed.

When I woke up to lovingly fix his CPAP as I had many nights before.

When I woke up and noticed he was in the same position from the last time I had woken up. When my heart knew what my mind did not want to believe.

Time arrives to the anniversary of my husband's passing.
Time brings me back to the present.

My mom had the most respectable memorial for my husband. I shortly realized how the cemetery staff believed my mom had lost her own son and looked confused when I was trying to explain she is my mom, my husband's mother lives outside of our country. The tombstone was in place for his anniversary of death.

I had written my husband a poem that I placed on his tombstone as a gift from my heart.

The field on the other side of beginnings and endings is where we will meet again.

I know it in my heart that we will meet again.

We will meet again so I can be sure to thank him once more for the life lessons, for taking care of my kids and me even in his absence, and for leaving with a good name and legacy of love.

We will meet again so I can yell at him for not doing enough in standing up to his birth family on my behalf. Contributing to their monstrous behavior and belief of superiority. Allowing them to walk all over us, believing he was taking the high road. I'm not being fair to my husband. His birth family never understood their own child was standing up for me by standing next to me with his silent language of taking the high road.

My mom had invited my husband's mother and father to this memorial. They were in Iran. My mom invited my husband's Uncle and his wife.

My husband's Uncle's wife tells me misunderstandings happen usually in weddings, funerals, and highly emotional events. Try to find love in your offended heart and resolve this issue with your husband's birth family.

I stood there thinking, I'm in so much physical pain I can hardly stand in front of you.
I stood there thinking, you don't know what happened. You are assuming it is a small misunderstanding.
I stood there thinking, haven't I heard this from you before?

I stood there in knowing that she is coming from Love and good intent.
I stood there in knowing I'm a loving person.
I stood there in knowing she has love in her heart as I.

So I told her that I do hope that all people who get offended by misunderstandings find peace and love in their hearts. I realize I confuse people with my offbeat statements.

Is it my place to educate people that bullying is different than misunderstandings and conflicts?
Is it my place to educate people in the art of live and let live?
Is it my place to educate people in the fallacy of making assumptions?

The memorial was loving. I was at first afraid of going to an event with my mom's friends when I was in so much pain. The loving energy of people consumed me. I realized I was glad to be there. I had now experienced an event for my husband's passing that was clear of the hateful, judgmental, and gossiping energy I had experienced in the year past.

It was a private event for my Tribe and my mom's friends who had shown her support in this tough year. My mom had asked me to invite my friends who had shown me support this past year.

I did not.
I could not even keep myself standing straight.
I did not have the bandwidth to do this simple task.

My kids all got sick yet again. My son's sickness was more severe. The fires in Southern California had consumed Santa Barbara County and the UCSB students had been evacuated from school. He had smoke damage in his lungs. He could not stop coughing. I was in so much pain myself that I couldn't even tend to my kids' needs. My younger sister comes to the rescue to heal my children. My older sister steps in to be the surrogate mother my kids so desperately required.

I am most grateful for my younger sister. Our healer. I am most grateful for my older sister. Our protector. Our caretaker. What would we do without her and her husband who have stepped in over and over to take on my family responsibilities?

They made sure I decorate my home for Christmas. They made sure we celebrate as we always had for the Winter Solstice and Christmas. They ensured Santa was there for my kids. My kids had an opportunity to sing songs and be merry.

My husband and my older sister's husband were both ski fanatics. A trip to Utah, my husband's American Hometown, was planned for the kids and me. A trip to ski with my older sister, her childhood friend "Spiritual Friend", and their husbands. I could not and would not get on the slopes. Not because my ski pant zipper wouldn't go up nor because my ski jacket was a tight fit. Really because I was still trying to walk straight without pain.

One night in Utah, while sitting in the living room of our suite with my older sister and Spiritual Friend, I was sharing how I am waiting for my younger daughter to turn 18 then I rather die and not live with all this pain. BANG. BANG. The three of us were startled. We walked into the bathroom to find the jets in the bathtub full of water running! We tried to turn it off to no avail. I immediately apologized to my husband and confirmed that I want to be around to see my great grandchildren. Can I just please do it without pain? At that moment, the jets stopped.

While in Utah, I sought out the Angel who sponsored my husband allowing him to come to the United States. I wanted our children to see him once more. I wanted to personally thank him again for playing a part in my privileged destiny. He had aged much since the last time I had seen him. Old age and illness were written on him. I had not realized what a creator he was. He showed us the tables he had made with poetry carved in them. He shared a book he had written. He was full of life in his frail now body.

I was striving for life in my broken body. We made it home and it was New Year's Eve. My Hostess Cousin and her husband suffered even more loss this year. They did not want to have a party. My sisters and I begged them, please let's have our lives go back to normal. Let's have a small party with family and friends. And for the love of us, they did.

The generous people that my Hostess Cousin and her husband are, they went through a lot of trouble to open their home, make food, and share it with love.

When my kids and I walked in, Childhood Friend was talking to my older sister. I walked up to join them. They both got quiet. I wondered what's up. They looked like they didn't want to tell me the something. I thought something I cannot bear has happened. Is it news of yet another loss? Then Childhood Friend said that my husband's siblings were invited tonight by mistake because they had been in the previous email lists. I shared my thought that they would never show up here. I guaranteed it. We have had this family tradition for over two decades. They have come less than a handful of times, only at the insistence of my husband.

Then my older sister mentioned that my husband's sister replied that she would not come. My husband's brother said that they might come depending on their jet lag. I shared my belief again. They would never show up here. I guarantee it. I walked away with confidence of this.

During the party, I found myself sitting with the many older women. Many of them had lost their husbands. So elegant, poised, and strong these women are. I was open to all the advice I was receiving. I listened to stories of how hard it is even after eight years. I listened to how I need to focus on my own individuality now. I listened to how I can't do it alone and will need my Tribe for the sake of my young kids.

I was up and walking around when suddenly Childhood Friend came to say, *They are all here, your husband's siblings with their spouses.* What? No. It can't be. I was in doubt. I was in confusion.

I walked away from Childhood Friend and right into the room nearest me. Unbeknownst to me, I walked into a room where the kids were having their own party. My younger daughter was on the floor playing cards with other young girls. My older daughter was laying on the bed of the room reading with Love Friend next to her. I was pleasantly surprised to see them.

I shared the news with my daughters. Your Uncle and Aunt are here if you'd like to go out and see them. They just looked at me. They were probably as shocked as I was. Then my older sister walked into the same room as us. She was looking for me. Wanted to ensure that I'm fine. I reassured her that I am. I just feel more safe and comfortable staying in this room. Then my son walked into the same room. *Mom, are you okay?* He goes straight into primal instinct of protection. Hugging me so I know he is here for me. I reassured him that it is all good. It is okay that they are here.

I sat on the bed with Love Friend and my older daughter. Love Friend held me as she loving massaged my older daughter's head. *This is not the venue for them to come for peace talks,* Love Friend shared. *If they want to work things out they should have called you to meet in private.*

I wondered, do they want peace talks? Is that why they came? That is stupid though. If they did, they wouldn't do it at a party. This is not a peace offering.

I wondered, are they here to show off to people how everything is okay? Take a few pictures and show off to social media that they were at my family party. That is stupid though. Why would they drive over an hour to do that?

I wondered, do they think that because they show up now everything from the past is fixed and forgotten? That is stupid though. We never go back to what was. We can only go forward to what will be. Are they stuck in wanting the past and not know how to get out?

Then I recalled the hardest lesson I'm still in the process of learning.

People don't think and act like me.
People think and act like themselves.

It occurred to me that what I consider stupid is different and not stupid to others. Maybe they figured they are invited and just showed up to have a good time at a party. Not caring that I would be here.

Rapidly, the room I was in became central station. Joy Cousin walked in with a tequila, crying. *I don't know what to do. I was told to serve this tequila to them.* I had to calm her. Let her know that I'm fine, go serve them tequila. They have a right to be at this party. They are guests here. I just need to be in this room now. Please go out there and have fun.

My Hostess Cousin came into the room crying. *I'm so sorry,* she keeps repeating to me. *I found out this morning about them having been invited and potentially coming.* She is truly devastated at this turn of events. I hug her to let her know it is okay. Please know I am fine. Just go out there and tend to your guests.

Childhood Friend stepped into the room to jovially tell me to write a Chapter and comically break any potential tension.

A drunken Fashion Friend came in to ask if she saw correctly, *Are they really here?* Making everyone laugh.

Helpful Cousin walked in to see what she can do for us.

Love kept walking into the room. Lovely People wanted to see if I was okay and make me feel more loved. Love wanted to be in the room where it happens.

Love Friend's husband, my cousin, came in to say *It looks bad that you are not coming out and just staying in this room.* He wanted me to know that he loves me and will do anything for me. He just doesn't want them to have ammunition to say anything bad about me. They might say that I came in the room to hide my kids from them.

Love Friend clarified for her husband that I had already given the option to my kids to go out and see their Uncle and Aunt. I wanted to ask my cousin, have they asked to see my kids?

Before I could, my older sister stepped in to take our cousin outside to talk and not in front of my kids. My older sister must have been tense and dumped it all on our cousin who had the love capacity to take it. I heard yelling. *Who cares what it looks like or what people say. She was caught off guard. She is protecting herself and her kids. She has every right to be where she feels safe.*

Just like that, my Hostess Cousin came in to say that they have left and to please come out of the room. *This party was meant to keep tradition for you and your kids.* I came out at her request. It was a real coming out for me.

Grounded in *groundedness*, I walked out and smiled at all the loving people looking at me and walked to the area where the older women were seated. I sat next to Childhood Friend's mother. I told her I am absolutely fine. I was only shocked. My mind knew that the expected behavior of me would have been to save face and exchange fake pleasantries with my husband's siblings. My heart told me to take myself out of a situation that I don't want to be in. I listened to my heart.

Childhood Friend's mother told me that this is an unfortunate situation. My deceased husband is the only person to blame here. If he had taken a strong stance with his family and stood up for me years ago, they wouldn't be so disregarding of me today.

Childhood Friend's mother shared her memory of her visit to Iran when my husband and I were dating. Childhood Friend's mother went to visit Good Looking Guy's parents at the request of my mom. My mom had wanted to see who the family of her daughter's boyfriend was. Childhood Friend's mother said they had no idea the two of us were seriously together and became standoffish.

This is true. My husband did not communicate anything to his family. And, he hated it when I did. Which I stopped doing at his request. And even if his family stepped all over us, he would never say a word to them thinking he was taking the high road. He couldn't have been further from his own parents' understanding and truth. He was avoiding any conflict. He couldn't handle conflict. He swept it all under the rug. I inherited the huge mess that has no beginning and God knows could ever have the ending of being cleaned up. I am a cleaner upper. Even for me, isn't it easier to walk away? It would take too much work and energy that I do not have the time and brain capacity for, to clean this mess. I have to protect my time and energy for moving my kids and I forward.

My Childhood Friend's mother wanted me to know the Herd does not have the courage to give me what I need. Recognition of wrongdoing. I know exactly what she is saying to me.

Life is the school.
Love is the lesson.
Compassion is the final exam.

We will be tested on showing compassion for ourselves, others, and those who challenged us in the giving of that compassion.

When my kids were young I would not ask them to share their toys. Instead, my focus was for my kids to feel secure in the ownership of their toys. My kids decided if they wanted to share and when. Eventually, my kids became the most benevolent in their toy sharing.

Could this be one of my life lessons?
Focus on me.
Take care of me.
Be respectful to me.

First, I need to feel secure with having compassion for myself before I can pass my final exam to fully show compassion to those who make it a challenge to be compassionate towards.

I understand that they are wounded beings.
I understand that I am a wounded being.
I understand I need to heal my *woundedness* in preparation for my final exam.

I tell my Childhood Friend's mother my hurt is too deep, the abuse went too far. I get she wants me to do well in my final exam. I understand my husband's birth family is incapable of remorse until the day they heal their *woundedness*. I have to respect my being and my needs. I have to show compassion to myself.

Because this was not a conflict to be resolved but rather a bullying situation, any initial outreach on my part would be welcoming back the status quo.

I do not want to walk back into an abusive relationship.
I will not walk back into an abusive relationship.
I will not risk a walk back into an abusive relationship.

I want to model strength for my kids.
I want to stand my ground with this.

I want my kids to grow up standing up for themselves.
I want my kids to grow up understanding the different meanings of compassion.

I wanted to make sure everyone had a good time and that the incident didn't impact anyone's evening. Only two years before, I had been on the dance floor with my husband. I went onto the dance floor to dance and show I'm in high spirits.

Even as I danced I was thinking, Childhood Friend's mother is correct that my husband's birth family has no respect for me. I am a child of God. I am of God. God is of me. Respect is my divine right. I easily give and receive the respect of so many loving people in my life. Really, my husband's birth family has never had respect for my parents or siblings either. Always giving the aura that they are better than.

As people started to leave, I felt secure in my realm of washing dishes and helped with clean up. My Hostess Cousin's husband came to talk to me. I figured he had invited them not by accident, but on purpose. He wanted me to know that they came extending an olive branch. They came because of me.

I had to know.
Did they ask to see me?
Did they ask to see my kids?
Apparently, they had not.

———

I told him that they came for show. To say, *look at how wonderful we are for showing up.* Could it be their parents made them come?

My Hostess Cousin's husband got upset at my judging. He was correct to be upset at my pettiness. *This is not who you are. You are not a person who would think they came for show. What happened to your compassion?*

He also had a holier image of me that I couldn't live up to. *They drove all the way here in spite of being jet lagged for a peace offering. They feel bad for the way they had treated you.*

I thought, should I take out the violin? I too drove all the way to your home after having driven 14 hours back from Utah the night before plus not being able to stand straight without pain. I did it to keep tradition for my kids.

I wanted to know.

Did they tell you they felt bad for the way they treated me? He indicated they didn't have to use words to say it. *They showed up tonight.*

I begged to differ. I was raped. I was spiritually raped. Just showing up is not a peace offering.

They didn't even ask to see my kids and me. They drove all the way here. The talk was they were just taking their typical selfies that I'm most sensitive to after my husband's funeral. They did not ask to see my kids.

Ask to see my kids? When will I learn? Why do I still ask for the impossible?

I had initially thought they had to fully understand their offenses committed. While standing in front of my Hostess Cousin's husband, I started to understand that I cannot expect the impossible.

I hugged my Hostess Cousin's husband knowing he is coming from a place of Love. He had wanted to make peace. He had fairy tale thoughts that the Herd would walk in, I would see them, and all would be well. We would live "Happily Ever After. The End."

Is that what my husband's parents thought when they invited my kids and me to that restaurant? The execution went wrong, the intent was right. Really, isn't it best if we all live outside of right and wrong in the world of live and let live? Let it be. Me included.

I needed to stop requiring the need for remorse from the Herd. I needed to stop hoping that they would ask to see my kids.

Was it my fault for not sharing my truth with my own Tribe? Was it my fault to not explain it was bullying and not a conflict?

If I had, would people still think it was a misunderstanding and that I being more understanding should show compassion? Aren't there different meanings and types of compassion? What about self-compassion?

I did feel bad for the Herd for making the long trip to this party. Was it bravery to show up? Or were they under the false impression that they would come to receive an apology from me for kicking them out of my home. After all, they were invited to my Tribe's territory.

Or were they just plain confused. Their behavior had not changed from the years past. Mine had changed by not accepting their behavior any longer.

My heart went out to my Hostess Cousin's husband for his breakdown on behalf of my husband. My heart went out to my Hostess Cousin for having to indicate a departure to bring back order and sanity into her home. My heart goes out to the Herd for possibly having good intentions and not executing properly. The whole matter sucked.

It sucked that egos are much too big.
It sucked that comprehensions are much too small.
It sucked that blame was the refuge of choice.

Once the evening was over, my sisters, their husbands, and I stayed up until 3 a.m. talking about life. My younger sister's husband informed us how we have grown up in a bubble of love that may have made us out of touch with the real world.

In the real world, people are not as loving. He also tenderly informed me that I should toughen up to elevate my worth. It was Rumi who said, "That which stirs you, is your worth." The day is going to come when I will run into my husband's birth family and I have to be able to not have it energetically affect me to the point that I go into hiding. I will have to rise above it.

My older sister's husband indicated that running into my husband's family in the street is different. This was a predatory act where I was caught off guard. I did not run away. I placed myself in a safe room to protect myself precisely because I know my worth. This shows strength.

I now realized that on the night that my husband's parents invited my kids and me to that restaurant, I should have not gone in after seeing Favorite Daughter-in-law in the parking lot. I should have left with my kids.

My husband's father broke our agreement. My only moral obligation was to my husband's parents and not his siblings. I kept my end of the agreement, not bringing my older sister and her husband around with me. How dare they walk all over me and catch me off guard by bringing their Herd to a dinner meant for grandparents and grandchildren?

The most heartbreaking part of this for me was that my husband's parents did not want to spend quality one on one time getting to bond with my kids.

Why am I heartbroken?

People don't love like me.
People love like themselves.

My younger sister and her husband for the first time that evening heard the stories of what I had endured. My younger sister's husband explained what "Bazari" had evolved to mean in the Persian language.

People whose operative is money.

They associate Love with money.
They associate Control with money.
They associate Respect with money.

Your husband's family is a clear case of being Bazari, though they are not Bazar Merchants.

The conversations went to my younger sister's husband's brother. With his divorce, my younger sister's husband and his mother willingly kissed the ass of the very difficult ex-wife to see their blood children. How my husband's siblings didn't have the decency to call the very kind hearted me even once this difficult year to say, *we would like to see your kids.* My husband's parents even turned down opportunities to see their own grandchildren to maintain power, to keep sanity within their egos.

The next morning, I saw my very delighted dad. He told me how proud of me he was that I was so smart to walk away into that room to not see the Herd. *Now people know not to mess with you. If your husband's family had half a brain they should realize that unless they come genuinely begging for your forgiveness for all they have done to you, and it may take many years of begging, they have no place in your life.*

My older sister was upset. She and her husband had worked so hard all of this difficult year to make sure my kids were feeling better each day and only have positivity around them. And then, just like that, there was regression. Five steps forward, two steps back.

My younger daughter had nightmares that night and for a while thereafter. Later, she told me that she had gone out for dessert at the party and my husband's brother, her Uncle, came up to talk to her and in that very short time snapped a picture with her.

Snapping a picture of my young daughter? Why?

They are either in or out. They can't be both.

They choose to be out when they choose to be disrespectful to me and my deceased husband.
They choose to be out when they choose to be abusive to me.
They choose to be out when they choose to be disrespectful to my birth family.

Maybe this needed to happen for me to realize that they are no longer my family. I do not have a physical husband, therefore I do not have a mother-in-law, father-in-law, brother-in-law, or sisters-in-laws. I am now a widow and a divorcee.

I have no regrets about separating from and now divorcing my husband's birth family.

Upon reflection, I realize I was not being rational. I was expecting remorse from people incapable of feeling remorseful in order for them to come back into my life. Rational thinking is that there is no space for them to be back in my life. I am done.

Maybe this night happened for me to have that change of heart. While before I had been open to my husband's siblings calling to see my kids, now I am no longer open.
Starting The Year of Me, I don't give a shit anymore for people who cannot respect me. My moral compass will still allow my kids' grandparents access when they ask, now with limitations I shall impose to deter the toxicity.

The stakes have now changed.

I dreamt I was on vacation with my husband and kids.
We were in a different place, far away.
We were staying at a vacation home that belonged to my parents.
My husband asked me to unclutter my mom's stuff.
I told him I'm on vacation and don't want to undertake this back breaking task.
He insisted that there isn't much opportunity for my parents to come all the way out to their vacation home and unclutter.
I should do as much as I can on their behalf while we are here.
Then it was time for us to travel back.
My husband left with our suitcases to join our kids who were waiting outside of the vacation house.
I was looking for the home key to lock up.
I couldn't find the key amidst the clutter.
I was realizing I should have listened to my husband and tidied the house for my mom.
My husband was anxious that we may miss our flight.
My husband waves to me to join him.
I finally found the key.
I walked out and locked the house door.
I turned around and see my husband's sister in front of me.

She starts to talk to me as if nothing has happened.
I looked at her in disbelief. Though I stand in silence, I am in rage.
What gives her the right to come and talk to me as if nothing has happened?
My husband calls out to me.
We need to go, don't dilly- dally. We have to make it to our flight.
I turn and run towards my husband and kids.
I woke up with utmost clarity.

My husband wants me to know.
He wants me to know my past is a key to know why I am who I am today.
He wants me to know my past is a key to know why I am where I am today.
He wants me to know I found the key to lock my door of the past.

I gift a keychain to my husband's mother for her 71st birthday.
May she find the key to her life.

My deceased husband is communicating with me.
Get rid of everything and everyone that does not serve you my love.
He wants me to rid myself of his family.
He wants me to fly high to my new life.

The Herd's offensive energy.
The Herd's massive ego.
The Herd's unconsciousness of truth.
It is not welcomed near me.
Not welcomed anymore near me.
Not welcomed anywhere near me.

I am getting rid of toxicity at a new level.
Out.
Get Out.
Get Out for Good.

I need not stupidity of ignorance.
I need not vanity of arrogance.
I need not negativity of jealousy.
I need not offense of disrespect.

I need not.
I will not be moved.
I Will not be moved.
I Will Not be Moved.

In The Year of Me...
I do not think of toxic others.
I cannot think of toxic others.
I do not have the bandwidth to think of toxic others.

What I will have in The Year of Me...

I will have Vitality as my divine right.
I will have Prosperity as my divine right.
I will have Respect as my divine right.

What I am in The Year of Me...

I am a happier me.
I am a tougher me.
I am a loving me.

What I will give in The Year of Me...

I will give Compassion to myself.
I will give Forgiveness to myself.
I will give Happiness to myself.

This was my husband's message.
Unclutter.

I had thought it was the physical objects in our home.
I had thought it was the thoughts in my mind.

Now I know it included an uncluttering of toxic people from my life.

Uncluttering from my husband's family.
I finally have arrived at letting go.
I finally am able to give it to Jesus.
I finally am able to praise Allah.

I can now forgive the Herd and release them.
I can now feel compassion for them and release them.
I can now wish the best for their lives and release them.

They have not been on my boat in this critical year.
They need not be in my physical life any longer.
There is only room for true loving energy in my life.

I love my deceased husband.
I love my kids.
I love my self.

I love my siblings.
I love my parents.
I love my sisters' husbands and children.

I love and adore my friends.
I love my neighbors.
I love my enemies.

I love my cousins.
I love my extended family.
I love my husband's family.

I love my ancestors.

I love all.

I love God.
I love Life.
I love Love.

My Vitality Plan

Rules
Eat 70 percent or more water based natural foods.
Eat 30 percent or less packaged foods.
No eating 12 hours after waking up.

Keep in Mind
No regrets.
Three bites of desserts should suffice.
Eat 2/3 of food in the first nine hours of the day.
Eat Slower. Chew More.
No more than two eggs per day.
Forgive Yourself. Love Yourself.

Guidelines
Am I going to regret eating/doing this?
If it doesn't taste good, three bites maximum.
If it tastes divine, three bites maximum.

Water
Drink half of your weight in ounces every day.
Add flavor such as lemon/lime, raw cranberry juice or cucumbers.

Supplements
Know the source of Vitamins.
General Health Vitamins.
Customized Vitamins based on individual body need.
Digestive enzymes.
Double Check body needs for Vitamin D, A and K2.

Stretch
Stretch in bed. Neck, Legs, Back, and Hands.

Breathing
Breath in < - > tummy should inflate out ; breath out <-> tummy should deflate in.
Active one minute breathing prior to each meal or snack.
Active breathing for body detoxification.

Sleep
Sleep a minimum of eight hours a night. Consistently.
Utilize sleep music.
Utilize guided meditation/music for sleep.
No electronics three hours prior to sleep.
Routines are important. (Hot Bath, Read a Book, etc.)
Essential Oils (Lavender).
Active 4-7-8 (breath in, hold, breath out) breathing prior to sleep.

Exercise
Use step monitoring device— measure steps on a daily basis
Cardio— three to five days per week.
Weight training— two days per week.

Food Tracking Tools
Weight Watchers App
MyFitnessPal App
FatSecret App

Affirmations
I'm open to all the health the universe has for me.
I am receiving. I am receiving now.
I am receiving all the health the universe has for me.

Vitality is my divine right.

I am a confident, disciplined person and will achieve anything I want.

Eating fresh, wholesome foods makes me look and feel great.

I love my life and every day of it is a blessing.

I have a charmed life and I have abundance of all things necessary to be happy and healthy.

Bathroom
Consistent time to poop everyday.
Observe urine color.
Observe stool texture.

Flossing
Can be done during the day at any opportunity, such as while driving.

Menu Options
Pre-Breakfast options:
(At wake up)
1 Cup of hot water with lime/lemon.

Breakfast options:
(Within 30 minutes of wake up)
1. Eggs
    a. 2 eggs any style
    b. 1 tsp oil
    c. 1-2 serving of veg.

2. Green Smoothie
    a. One to two servings of fruit or frozen fruit.
    b. One to two servings of vegetables.
    c. Protein Powder.
    d. Almond milk, yogurt, or water.

    e. Kale or Spinach.
    f. Saffron.
    g. Bee Pollen.
    h. Chia Seeds.
    i. Flaxseed Oil.

3.   Lentils
    a. Recipe: Soak for 24 hours. Stir fry onions first. Add one cup of lentils to three cups of broth or water. Boil until ready to eat.

4. Hot Cereal covered with Honey or Fruit.

Mid-Morning Snack options:
(2-3 hours after breakfast)

1. Ten RAW (not roasted) Nuts with one fruit serving.
2. Cottage Cheese with fruits.
3. 0.5 oz. of Pumpkin Seeds.
4. 1 oz. of any RAW Nuts (Almonds, Walnuts, etc.)
5. 5-6 Macadamia Nuts.
6. Yogurt with cucumbers.
7. Greek Yogurt with Fruit.
8. Two tablespoons of nut butter with celery.

Lunch options:
(2-3 hours after Mid-Morning Snack)

1. Protein with Salad and/or Vegetables or Soup:
a.   Pamper yourself with dressings or sauces.
b.   Treat yourself to ½ cup of rice/quinoa grain.

Afternoon Snack options:
(2-3 hours after Lunch)

1. Greek Yogurt with Veggies (Cucumber, Spinach, etc.).
2. One cup of Edamame.
3. Green Smoothie.

4. Two Hard Boiled Eggs (Can not have if breakfast was eggs).
5. Cottage Cheese with Nuts.
6. Up to 12-Tortilla Chips and Salsa (Not the best option, doesn't hold you over).

Dinner options:
(2-3 hours after Afternoon Snack)

1. Protein with Salad and/or Vegetables or Soup:
a. Pamper yourself with dressings or sauces.
b. Treat yourself to ½ cup of rice/quinoa grain.

After Dinner Option:
(If necessary- Not preferred)

1. One Serving of Fruit or Endless Servings of Vegetables.

Chapter Sixteen
ExVolution

RESPECT
RESPECT
RESPECT
RESPECT
RESPECT
RESPECT
RESPECT

I've been told that the second year of loss is much harder than the first.
The first year is a daze.
The second year, the hardships of life begin to hit.
The second year, the fog disappears and hurt is deeply felt.

When our son was born, we realized how life slowed down and how hard it was to keep it all together. For example, being on time was becoming more of a challenge. Then our older daughter was born and it hit us like a hurricane. Having had one child was a breeze, having two was difficult.

I concur that most of my first year of loss was a daze. I had been in a state of observance of my surroundings. I really couldn't get myself to do too much of anything for emotional reasons. My husband used to check our mail. It takes an emotional toll on me to do what he used to do, unless I'm pretending he is on business travel and that is why I'm checking the mail.

I have to stop pretending in my mind that he is away temporarily.
I have to accept that he is not coming back.
His clothes in our closet won't be worn.
I have to face reality. Or reality will hit me in the face.

Some days are so hard to handle and some days are just fine. And it is never the days that I anticipate. There was so much anticipation for birthdays.

My Kids' first birthdays without their dad.
My birthday without my husband.
And his 50th birthday when many loved ones called me to say they were thinking of my kids and me.

My hardest day was the first day of school. My husband used to take our kids to school. He had a tradition of taking pictures of them and singing a special song in the car ride to school. As I had made lunches and was ready to walk out the door my kids asked, *Aren't you going to take a picture?* Reminded that it was the first day of school, my heart broke. I held myself together through the taking of pictures and singing in the car. After drop off, I fell apart in one of the worst days of my grieving life.

I realize that my husband was the math genius. He was the one who always engaged with our kids for their academic achievements. I realize I have nothing in this area to offer my kids. Even when I know how to, I am now not able to answer a math question or help with any homework. I ask the girls to call their brother for help. Then, I feel guilty. My son has his life and should not be burdened with what he was lucky enough to have his father here for.

It was my husband's job to ensure our son came home by his curfew. Staying up by myself to wait for my older daughter to drive back home from a party is torture. I have never failed to stop tearing in having to take the role of my husband with our kids. I wish my husband would be here to consult with. What am I to do when my older daughter tells me she will be home by 11 p.m. and by 11:30 p.m. she is still not home?

What am I to do when I am in severe pain of my broken rib when it is late at night and younger daughter approaches me because her body has been invaded by hives? There is no allergy medicine in our medicine cabinet. I am overwhelmed with tears.

I am overwhelmed.
I am overwhelmed my husband is not here to share the burden of raising our kids.
I am overwhelmed because of the emotional energy attached to things my husband did that now I am responsible for.

Will this subside?
Will I know when it has subsided?

Why am I an Only Parent?
Why did I become an Only Parent?
Am I now envious of Single Parents?

I go back to gratefulness.
I am grateful to be an American.
I am grateful to have experienced my loss in our great nation
where my children cannot be taken from me and we are
protected under our laws.
I am grateful to have been surrounded by a culture of friends
that collected money and gave useful gifts in my time of need.
I am grateful to have been brought food to my home in my
time of grief instead of abiding a tradition to go out with
people to eateries.
I am grateful to have been shown useful love and belonging by
my community and neighbors.
I am grateful that Helpful Cousin lives close by and helps with
school pickups.
I am grateful that my neighbor brought my younger daughter
allergy medicine, late in that night, in my hour of pain.
I am grateful that we are a nation of service.
I am grateful that we embody doing good for others vs. talking
about doing good to look good to others.

I am grateful for belonging to my American Family.
I am grateful for belonging to my Iranian-American Family.
I am grateful for belonging to my Humane Family.

Belonging—

We all belong together. In our abundant world, there is space
for every one of us. We are all here for the purpose of teaching
one another skills to evolve our humanity. Even though on the
surface it seems as if we are not accepting of one another, at
our core we are in need of one another.

How can we ensure we send the feeling of belonging to our fellow beings?

By Listening.
By learning from answers to asked questions.
By Knowing.
By taking the time to learn the person.

As a young scared adolescent having just learned to drive, I was stopped at a red traffic light. A homeless person walked the crosswalk. Not knowing, I locked my car door. He gave me the look of being misunderstood. I will never forget his stare into my eyes. I immediately realized what a demeaning act I had just perpetrated. In that moment of shame for my misunderstanding, I learned the life lesson of belonging. We all belong. In my life, I have made it a practice to stop and talk to all. Sitting in a fancy restaurant or sitting at a street corner, we all belong.

I stop, kneel, and look in the eye of a homeless woman sitting on the corner of a San Francisco street. I ask her how she is holding up in the cold. She shows me how she keeps warm. I listen to her. I look her in the eye and acknowledge her. I recognize how clever and creative she is for the cardboard boxes she has pulled together to keep warm. I take the time to leave her and go to a drug store so I can return to hand her pads for menstruation, a towel so she can keep dry, protein bars, and water. Warmly caressing her hands as she accepts.

I have now learned to have a homeless kit for women and a homeless kit for men to carry in my car that I can hand out when stopped at a street corner where there is a need. I draw a heart on the paper bag that houses the necessities I provide.

My brother is bipolar. I see how without the care of family, my brother may be on the street begging for money to survive. I see how without the care of family, my brother may be on the street yelling and talking to himself. I see how without the care of family, my brother may feel like he doesn't belong. I see how I am family to my brother and to all human beings.

Being Enough—

Wouldn't life be wonderful if as humans we all knew we were enough?

Not all those who don't feel enough assault.
All those who assault don't feel enough.

I strongly feel that those who assault others need to prove themselves because they do not feel they are enough.

How can we ensure we send the feeling of being enough to our fellow beings?

By Seeing.
By recognizing what is done well.
By Saying.
Giving specific authentic compliments.

Gifting the power of positive reinforcement can be one the most healing acts for our collective progression. So many of us are in need of recognition. So many of us are in limbo about purpose in our lives.

As a young adult, I don't recall having the luxury of discovering my purpose prior to making life decisions. I lived life with the flow of it. I knew I had to study, finish school, get a job, get married, start a family, and build a life. I never stopped to question this path.

I did always keep an eye out for what my purpose is as life was happening. I got good at formalizing a life mission for myself: To have a positive impact on the lives of people around me by sharing an abundance of knowledge, wealth, and happiness. I formalized a purpose for myself: Respect. Love. Grow.

I can see in my son how young adults today question it all in advance of making their life decisions. I can see how more young adults today have the luxury of making a difference in the world. This confidence of trust in their future is a direct result of knowing you are enough. A parent, teacher, and/or community member recognized their goodness by giving them relevant positive reinforcement. Making sure they knew they were enough. Now they can go and have a positive impact in the world.

Gratefulness—

It is miraculous, the power of gratefulness. Even though it is not a tool to change our destiny, it is a tool to guide us en route to becoming Spiritual Beings.

As Animals we live in fear.
As Spiritual Beings we live in trust.
Living in Gratefulness is practice for living in trust.

How can we ensure grateful living?

By Asking.
Simply asking others what they are grateful for activates trust in our fellow beings.
By Writing.
Writing what we are grateful for activates trust in our own beings.

I don't know how I would have survived this year of loss without gratefulness. Forcing myself to write what I'm grateful for. For simple blessing such as having eyes to see and having shoes to wear. I asked my kids what they were grateful for every day and what was going right in their lives. I made them think and tell me what blessing they have. I made them think and tell me what they did right.

Focusing on our blessings has been giving my kids and me reinforcement that a higher power is taking care of us and all of our needs. Faith and Hope are what has kept us going in this difficult year.

Over and over, I am grateful to be a part of this life.
I am grateful that my amazing family has had by back.
I am grateful that I have amazing friends.
I am grateful that I had spent the time spent with my husband.
I am grateful that I had spent the time spent with my husband's family.

In my soul searching to see what part I had played in becoming a target for Family Bullying, I discovered that I failed in belonging.

I had always been grateful for my husband's parents' generosity.
I had always been grateful when they spent time with my husband and kids.
I had always been grateful to my husband's mother for my life lessons learned.

I had never felt like I belonged with them. Eventually, I did not want to belong with the Herd.

Was it me, not them?
I could not relate to what I viewed as inauthentic living.
I chose not to take part.

This must have caused the rage in them towards me.

Or was the rage a primal instinct that the majority of the traditional world experiences? Thus the laws in some countries that rip one of the most oppressed women's groups in the world, Widows, of Human Rights.

Even when laws are put in place to protect Widows, some countries' culture will allow communities to attack Widows by ripping them of their children, property, and dignity. In the most advanced countries, Widows lose their main breadwinners and likely lose social status and potentially fall into poverty. Even in the United States, primal instinct attacks of a sophisticated nature on Widows are known to happen across race, culture, and socioeconomic status.

Still, we are so blessed that in our young country, we have laws and a culture of love, care, and giving to the downtrodden.

I had repeatedly told my husband's father that they did not see me as a part of their family. The truth is that I had not seen myself as a part of their family. I never felt comfortable being around or with them.

I passed judgment for their attachment to material objects and external beauty.
I passed judgment for their feeling of superiority.
I passed judgment for their inability to comprehend the way I did.

I forgive myself for judging. The truth is that I don't know how life should be for our collective highest good.

I have learned that my husband's family may never accept their offenses committed. I have learned to forge forward and live my life.

I have relief and salvation.
I have realities and facts.
I have opportunities and success.

My heart is truthful and I love God with a pure and benevolent aim.

I am now proud of myself for my intuition. I had always been and am trusting of my feelings.
I realize that although my childhood visions had subsided, they had not completely disappeared. I had seen my husband's brother's difficult life in my vision. Favorite Daughter-in-law was right. At an unconscious level, I may had hoped that my husband's brother would take a different path.

Destiny is destiny and cannot be interfered with.
Caring is also caring and cannot be stopped.

When I dig deeper, I had the vision at my young age of 17 of becoming a widow, when my Childhood Friend's father passed away. I saw myself in Childhood Friend's mother. I saw my future in Childhood Friend's mother.

I had also had a few dreams of being unmarried throughout my marriage. I recall waking up confused and only in physically seeing my husband next to me did I realize it was only a dream.

I recall as a teenager hearing President Reagan refer to Iranians as *Barbaric*. My heart broke. How can a leader be so unworthy and unevolved? How can a leader promote hate?

I became super sensitive to any negative portrayal of Iran and Iranians. I became super sensitive to any negative portrayal of Islam and Muslims. I became super sensitive to negative portrayal of any subgroup of Americans.

Not all Iranians are Muslims.
Not all Muslims are Iranian.
Not all Humans are Humane.

I remember a conversation with my Italian-American boss as an older teenager at a summer internship I had for The City of Monterey. I communicated with her that being Italian is the "it" factor. She was surprised by this discovery. Most popular kids in my high school were of Italian descent. Being an Iranian is looked down upon in our society. She shared that when she was in high school being Italian was looked down upon in Society. If this is the case, then tides change. The day will come when being Iranian-American will be the "it" factor. She had me promise to share my story with a young immigrant teenager so they know that tides will change for them as well. That time seemed like a long way away.

Then came the book NOT WITHOUT MY DAUGHTER. I did not buy it. I did not want to read it. Then came the Movie with the same title. I did not see it. I did not want to see it. I was disgusted at how Hollywood sensationalized and promoted hatred of Iranians and Muslims. This hatred in movies had been promoted at every turn for the past forty years of my awareness regarding this matter.

Who are the powers at be that promote Muslim hatred?
Who are these humans that promote hatred?
What is their game?
What is their gain?

I share this because I love Iran. It feels treasonous for me to write about the lack of human rights in a country I adore. It feels treasonous for me to write about the lack of respect in a country I adore.

Having been brought up in a small town where my parents were happy to drive 30 plus miles to spend time with other Iranian-Americans, I hadn't realized how I would fall in love with Iran's culture and history as an American adult.

Mesopotamia: the cradle of civilization.
Persian Empire: the largest empire ever established.
Iran: the land of culture and history.

From the people of this land is where civilization as we know it today was formed through developments in philosophy, religion, law, science, and technology.

The Persian Empire created the concept of States (istan). Countries today such as Uzbekistan, Turkmenistan, and Afghanistan all had been self-governing States within the Persian Empire.

Because of its vastness, the Persian Empire was home to many religious beliefs and three of the four known races of the time. Blacks, Whites, and Yellows all came together to mix in this Utopia of existence.

We in the United States have the advantage of the Red race for a complete human existence of mixtures. We in the United States also like to dumbify our society.

Labeling a race with the continent of Asia.
Labeling a race with the religion of Judaism.
Labeling a race with the culture of Hispanic.

Then giving a new definition to race— race groups to match what we have done.

I get it. We have a dark history and created the negative word associations made with the words Red, Yellow, and Black in the United States thanks to separatists in our land.

Categorization? Human Race. Aren't we all a mixture by this day and age anyway? What is this obsession with categorizing?

I love saying I'm American. There is not much one can do with the words United States to describe oneself. I'm United Statesian? So American it is.

America includes the entirety of our great continent of America- the Red, White, Black, Yellow, Brown, Orange, Purple, and the entirety of colors. Please say you are Asian if you currently are from Russia, Saudi Arabia, India, Japan or a country in the continent of Asia, and are only in the United States for a visit. If you are from the United States, you are American and not Asian.

Most of the world says there are five continents.
Asia. Europe. America. Africa. Oceania.

We say there are seven continents. Asia. Europe. Splitting America. Africa. Splitting Oceania into islands we include in Asia, then Antarctica, and Australia.

Let's stop at some point and ask what are facts?
How and by who are ideas we live by created?
Do we follow even if it doesn't make sense?
Do we follow when it makes sense?

Is United States under Canada? Or is United States under Mexico?
Is England the center of the world thus creating a Far East? Middle East? Western World?
Is Alexander the Great called "the Great" because of Cyrus the Great?

How did Cyrus the Great bring together people of different religious beliefs and races? By creating the first ever known Declaration of Human Rights. People had the right to practice their own religions without persecution. An example is the Jewish religion's celebration of Chanukah and gratefulness for being saved and protected under Cyrus the Great.

In the Persian Empire, slavery did not exist. All workers that built Empire buildings such as Persepolis thousands of years ago were fairly paid.

Unfortunately, we cannot say the same in the building of our Capital in Washington D.C. hundreds of years ago. What we can say is that Thomas Jefferson was a fan of Cyrus the Great and borrowed a great many concepts for the creation of our United States of America Constitution.

What was done in Iran to unite people of different creeds? Celebrating Seasons. Yes, it has roots in the Zoroastrian faith. One of the oldest practicing religions of our time that gave us Positive Thoughts, Positive Words, Positive Deeds.

The change of Seasons became a celebration that united all. The beauty of it is that the seasons change at the same exact moment for everyone on earth. We could take note and start to celebrate our Earth by celebrating our seasons.

Why are we celebrating an arbitrary Earth Day in April? The occurrence of the spring equinox should be the Earth Day celebrated by all of us. Not an arbitrary day that had been associated to an animalistic man who had killed his pregnant girlfriend.

Spring, the first known season to all of humanity. People all over the world, without the technology of communication, celebrated the spring equinox as a form of the first of the year for their people. The clues are for our taking. *September* is the 7th month. *October* is the 8th month. *November* is the 9th month and *December* is the 10th month. The numbering of these months indicates that the month of the beginning of spring, March, is the start of the calendar year, as celebrated in today's Iran.

Iran is a Nation of resilience. When invasions occurred, Persians embraced welcoming the new cultures and acclimating. Persians stood strong in keeping their celebration of seasons though in conflict with Abrahamic religions that saw it as Pagan practices.

Another example of this resilience is modern day Persian that is mixed with words from languages of Iran's invaders. Spoken Persian was kept alive after the Arabic conquest in the seventh century. However, Persian script was lost to Arabic Script in this time.

Farsi is how you say Persian, in Persian.
Deutsch is how you say German, in German.
Española is how you say Spanish, in Spanish.
This is verified by the Naval Postgraduate and Defense Language Institute Foreign Language School (DLIFLC).

Iran is now a nation of a broken home. Maybe bad karma has taken the nation to where it is today. It used to be a nation with a Mother, Farah the Great, and a Father, the Shah (King). Some viewed the Shah as a reminder of how the United States toppled Iran's democracy and criticized the SAVAK's torture practice under the Shah, guided by the United States' CIA. Others saw parents of strength who did their best to care for the wellbeing of their nation. Parents who sacrificed their own wellbeing and stepped in to protect a country whose oil would have been exploited regardless of who the leaders were. The 1978 revolution turned into a shit-volution. Without caring parents, Iran has become a broken home.

Ungratefulness is a poison that kills.
Thinking you know better than, is a poison that kills,
Thinking you are better than, is a poison that kills.

God bless the karma of the United of States of America.
God forgive us our sins of acting as a bully in the world.
God forgive us our sins of taking lives from the world for financial gain.

The truth is that we do not know what the future holds for the United States.

The truth is that we are a young nation. As we mature, our life cycle will be unveiled.

Iran is a mature nation that ruled in its younger years and now has been raped by the taking of its most precious resources for the personal gain of foreign citizens. Iran is a nation that has been stripped of its dignity. Iran is a nation that yearns for RESPECT.

It yearns for Citizens respecting one another by not stealing.
It yearns for Citizens respecting their land by not littering.
It yearns for Citizens respecting themselves by not lying.

Respect has different definitions for different people.

That was our family agreement. RESPECT. The five of us signed it. We wrote out our family agreements when my son was in fifth grade thanks to my son's fifth grade teacher at McAuliffe, the most wonderful school on earth.

Respect
-Property, objects, and family.
-Everything, living and nonliving.

That was our simple family agreement.

As Nations have their Karma so do family units.

It was the Karma of my family unit that has us where we are today, husbandless and fatherless.

It was the Karma of my family unit that has me where I am today, a survivor of predatory behavior.

It was the Karma of my family unit that has my kids where they are today, resilient.

I go back to soul search. Dignity.

Dignity—

A person who has perpetrated predatory behavior should NOT feel Shame.
Every person is acceptable on earth and here for a purpose.

A person who has perpetrated predatory behavior should feel Guilt.
Every aware person on earth feels remorse for bad behavior.

There is abundant empathy and love for those who are predatory in behavior. There is understanding for those who feel less than and must assault.
There is graciousness for those who have the courage to admit transgressions.

When there is NO remorse there is NO relationship.

I know life is complicated.
Sometimes you have to maintain a relationship despite repeated assault.
Sometimes you have to maintain a relationship despite existence of remorse.

Stand Strong. Have the courage to verbalize it to your predator.
Have the courage to say NO.
Have the courage to yell Get OUT.
Have the courage to throw their words in your garbage can and not into your physical being.

I can feel compassion without physically allowing predators with no remorse into my life. I can dig into my place of strength in dealing with predators. The day will arise for me to dig into my place of love in dealing with predators.

Yes. A person who assaults is not enough and feels less than.
Yes. A person who assaults is from a place of fear in evolution.

———

Yes. A person who assaults is from not belonging to the human family.
Yes. A person who assaults is not grateful for what is.

If we can all learn, know, and see this, we may be able prevent predatory behavior.

If we have been predatory in behavior, knowing that it is our behavior that was bad and not our being, we may be able to find salvation.

We are brilliant for recognizing our actions.
We have the ability to be remorseful for our transgressions.
We have the power to dig deep and find the courage to be vulnerable.

We all have a responsibility to move forward in our collective evolution.

As the great nation of service that we are, let's learn about each other and move forward with RESPECT.

We respect what we love.
We love what we know.
We know what we learn.

Closure

Another spring equinox approached and with it came my husband's family. I received a phone call from my husband's father that they are in the United States and needed to see me. I was very strict in my communication with him.

What do you need to see me for?

We need to talk about relations.

You are more than welcome to say what you want on the phone. I'm listening now.

We need to talk in person.

If it were important for you to communicate, you would tell me now on the phone.

Will you meet us at a cafe?

I will not.

Will you come over and visit us now that we are in the United States?

I will not.

I have your Tehran apartment title that I would like to give to you.

I appreciate that you brought it. Please mail the title to me.

I will not mail such an important document. Please come to my daughter's home or meet us at a cafe to pick it up.

I will not. You can place it at my front door if you'd like.

We need to see you and talk in person.

In order to end this tennis match, I offered my availability on Tuesday from 4-5 p.m. at my home. This is a time they can visit in person and drop off my Tehran apartment title. I ended the conversation letting them know that if they do not come on Tuesday at 4 p.m., I will assume that they have left my title by my front door.

Coming to my home to visit me was beneath their stature. They felt like they took the high road to make such a visit.

I had asked my girls to be present in order to see their grandparents, though their grandparents had not asked to see them. Only my older daughter made the time for their visit. I had asked Pillar Friend and my dad to be there for moral support.

The visit in short was to inform me that I must do "the right thing" and go to their daughter's home to visit my husband's birth family. My husband's mother told me that she is here for testing due to an abnormality discovered in her lungs. Also, my husband's father told me how wonderful they are for bringing me my Tehran apartment title. I was also informed that I would be unable to accomplish anything in Iran without their help. And again there was the same talk about how the various units of the apartment belong to them and my kids and that zero units belong to me. I was informed that if I chose not to deal with my husband's parents now, I would have to deal with their son and daughter upon their deaths.

All the while I was thinking, why don't they offer to transfer their portion to my son or me. This would be the only way that my hard earned money, wrongly invested in Iran, would not end in my husband's siblings' hands due to Iranian laws.

I stood up on the hour at 5 p.m. to thank them for their visit. This was a sign of my disrespect from their point of view. This was a sign of my self-respect from my point of view. I meant business in my dealings with them.

As we said our goodbyes, their continued focus was on teaching me etiquette. I "must" visit them in their daughter's home. My response to this was that my home door has and will always be open for them to come and visit my kids. My older daughter took offense to their air of superiority that her mother needed etiquette lessons.

The fact that I did not take the initial steps to follow up with any phone calls or visits irritated them. I realized this. I was en route to energetically separate myself from them. I had written pages upon pages for my healing. Rereading my pages of *Survivor Benefits* initially made me shake uncontrollably and eventually made me cry with a deep heartache that has finally made me strong and resilient.

A friend of my husband's father called requesting to visit me. I absolutely had no time for this nonsense.

My business had lost money in my year of loss and I was 100% focused to turn my financial life around. I was asset rich and cash flow *poortential*. My focus was to make enough money for my kids and I to survive. In a blink of an eye, my younger daughter will turn eighteen and my survivors benefits would come to an end.

On the phone, I was once again strict in my communication by forcing my husband's father's friend to give me a valid reason for his desire to steal my precious time with a visit. He did not give me a purpose for his desired visit nor did he make such a visit.

My younger daughter's birthday approached. She insisted on inviting her grandparents. I made it clear that she is free to do so. However, she needs to pick up the phone and call her grandparents herself. She did. My younger daughter called and invited her grandparents to visit her for her birthday. I was elated on behalf of my younger daughter that they had accepted to come.

My husband's parents were dropped off at my home. I was happy for my younger daughter to spend time with her grandparents. My mom came because she wanted to see my husband's mother and find out about the testing that was done on her lung. My mom kept the conversation going as is normal for her, yet she did not get a clear answer with regards to the results of the lung test. I finally got up to thank and hug my mom goodbye. I had wanted my younger daughter to have quality time with my husband's parents who had been generous enough to accept her invitation and brought her and my older daughter their usual generous birthday gifts.

I had specifically told them that we would be celebrating with a birthday cake. My younger daughter asked them to play cards with her and her sister prior to having cake. It hadn't even been five minutes that they were playing cards that my older daughter came to me while I was in the middle of taking care of laundry.

Dad's sister is here.
I was confused and shocked. My husband's sister is inside our home?

I came out to where they were playing cards. I realized that my husband's sister was sitting in her car in front of our home waiting. I was furious on behalf of my younger daughter. They had only been at our home for a little over half an hour. They hadn't even spent five minutes with their granddaughter who had the heart of courage to call and invite them.

Probably realizing that my husband's sister was not going to be offered to enter into our home, they were quick in wanting to leave. I reminded them that I had a cake and my younger daughter had hoped to celebrate with them. My husband's mother agreed for me to bring out the cake and watch my daughter blow out her candles.
As we all gathered around the kitchen island, I was trying to light candles on my younger daughter's cake when my husband's father started to attack.

How it is my fault that my son is not returning his phone calls. I stopped him and informed him that not everything is my fault. Please refocus. We are here now to celebrate my younger daughter.

My husband's mother chimed in to calm the situation saying that *everything will work out.*

My heart stirred.
My worth got challenged with those words.
Everything will work out?
My being was affected energetically.

I shared my thoughts with my husband's mother. Your every day lives are the same and not affected. It is my life that has changed forever. Everything might work out for you, but it will not for me. Not without my husband. I gave an example of my pain. My younger daughter is graduating eighth grade. My husband was here for my son and older daughter's eight grade graduations. He will not be here for my younger daughter. How will everything work out?

Words Spoken.
Meanings misunderstood.

My older daughter brought focus back to my younger daughter singing her Happy Birthday. As the cake was frantically cut and hardly eaten, they were out the door.

My younger daughter criticized me for jumping at my husband's parents. My older daughter brought back focus for my younger daughter explaining that it was their grandfather who had attacked me. I was merely standing up for myself and my girls should be proud of that. She also brought to light for her younger sister that it was her special day and they had not wanted to spend anytime with them bonding. Less than five minutes of playing cards and then leaving. Their grandfather's only concern is his grandson, their brother. My older daughter explained to my younger daughter that their grandfather had ruined the cake experience because all he cared about was their older brother.

This visit became the turning point for my younger daughter. She was able to let go. In the months to come, I realized the immense transformation in her. After a year and a half, she was finally happy again. She grew closer and more loving towards to me. I also did cave in and adopted a rescue dog for her. I'm in love with Tanner, our Rottweiler, even though he is a lot of work.

Fashion Friend called me to say she had another dream.
Fashion Friend was in the back seat of her car and her husband was driving with the passenger seat empty.
Fashion Friend and I were talking on the phone.
My heart was heavy and she was listening.
Suddenly my husband appeared in the passenger seat and could only be noticed by Fashion Friend.
My husband grabbed the phone from Fashion Friend to listen to what I was saying. I was under the impression I was still talking to Fashion Friend.
I finally finished talking. My husband told me, "Everything will work out".
Fashion Friend woke up.

Fashion Friend and I had not spoken for so long. She had no idea my husband's parents were in the country and had visited. What did this dream mean? My husband in a dream repeats the exact words his mother had shared with me earlier.

———

My husband's father called to tell me how evil I am. How I have kept my son away from him. How I need to "order" my son to call him. My heart ached for my husband's father. He had lost his son as I had my beloved husband. His wife's state of health was uncertain. I saw his outreach as a cry for help. I wanted to help him.

I explained to him that he needed to look into the mirror to see what he can do differently so that he can win the hearts of his grandchildren. He took offense to my statement. He started to attack me some more. Saying I was a liar and nothing I said had validity.

I kept my worth above his attacks. I explained to him that if I had grandchildren I would go to the ends of the world to have them in my life. They are a mere five miles from my home and didn't even want to spend five minutes with their granddaughters. He proclaimed that my words had no legitimacy.

The next day, my son called to inform me that my husband's parents and sister were in Santa Barbara to visit him. Wow. They did go to the ends of the world for the one grandchild, my son.

My son met them at a cafe. My son recounted that they acted as if nothing had happened. They offered to take him to a car dealership of his choice to buy him a car. He refused. He informed them that he did not wish to receive from people who were disrespectful to his mother. My husband's sister translated on his behalf that *while he has not seen it with his own eyes, his mother claims that we have been disrespectful to her.* Though my son is not fluent in Persian, he corrected his aunt, stating that he had in fact seen the level of disrespect with his own eyes.

Nonetheless, my husband's father replied that *if your mother feels that she has been disrespected, we apologize to you.* My son thought, *what in the world? You should apologize and show remorse to my mother, not to me.*

My son then informed them that they are playing favoritism with him and he does not wish to isolate his sisters. My husband's father went on to say that they are doing everything in the world for his sisters and are giving so much love to them. *If you feel that we need to do more for your sisters, we will do it for you.*

My son was handed an envelope upon leaving. He opened the envelope that evening to find a check for fifteen thousand dollars. Who does that? Give so much money to a new nineteen-year-old. I was frustrated on behalf of my son to have such a load placed upon him. He refused to accept the check. As solid as my son is in his convictions, he felt that accepting such a gift was a slap in the face of us four as one unit.

My husband's parents then made a visit to my parents' home. It was the same story. A visit to complain about evil me who had not initiated calling or visiting them.

My dad had had enough.

My dad made it clear that they are not to put down his humane daughter again. They surely had no right to visit my parents' home for the purpose of putting down their bereaved daughter.

My mom had had enough.

My mom wanted them to understand that despite all that they had done, I still had an open door policy for them visiting their grandchildren. It is their loss for not wanting to take advantage of such an opportunity.

318

My mom wanted them to understand that I was fully supported in my decision to never step into their daughter's, my husband's sister's, home ever again. *You want to complain about my daughter not initiating contact with you? Do you even know what garbage your daughter talked about one day after our beloved son-in-law's passing? Claiming he had stolen money from his own birth family. Do you know that Favorite Daughter-in-law had the audacity to repeat the same garbage to a mutual friend?*

My husband's father, clearly taken by surprise, started attacking my mom. *Are you accusing my son of stealing money from me?* At this point, my mom realized she is dealing with irrationality. My husband's mother started to cry. She then said that my husband was her most honest, honorable, and humane child.

My dad mentioned how paranoia kills gratefulness. It is too bad that they could not be grateful for the life his daughter and their son had created.

My dad asked everyone to shake hands and kiss cheeks so that they could leave his home in peace. The time had come to leave.

My husband's father called to tell me that they want to see my daughters "per my son's request" prior to leaving back for Iran in the coming week. However, I must bring them to his daughter's/their home. I refused to take them there. I had thought the intent should be being with my kids. The intent should not be for me to succumb and visit their home. He had a choice to visit my kids at my home. He did not.

At this point, my intuition desired reaching out to my husband's mother. I wanted to make sure she had a chance to visit my girls even though her husband had rejected his own outreach to see my girls.

319

I called my husband's mother. I inquired about her health. She informed me that it was in fact lung cancer that had already spread to her brain. I was wounded by the news.

True to my being, I openly shared my feelings with her. I told her that I loved her for she had brought my soul mate into the world. How I had done all that I could to be the best wife possible for her son, the best mother possible for her grandchildren, and even the best daughter-in-law possible for her.

I told her how I had evolved as a human being because of my interactions with them. How I was grateful for this and to her for all my life lessons. She seemed taken off guard and speechless at my outpouring of verbal love. She then replied that she loved me too.

My heart was exploding.

I asked if she would like to come visit her granddaughters prior to going back to Iran. She wasn't sure. I offered to meet her at a cafe or pick her up and bring her over to my home if it would be difficult for her to come on her own. She asked me if the invitation was being extended to only her and not her husband. Yes, I explained. I needed to have positive energy around me and I couldn't invite attacks into my home and life. She then said *No*. She would not come to visit my girls prior to her return to Iran.

I started to sob.
I'm not sure why I was crying.

Was I crying for my kids?
Was I crying for my loss?
Was I crying for an end?

She tried to make me feel better by telling me that she had lots of shopping to do prior to her trip and just didn't have the time for a visit. Of course, they had the time to drive over four hours to visit my son in a cafe for half an hour. She did not have the time to drive five miles to visit my girls? I forgave my thoughts of judgment and went back to love.

I told her, from my place of love, that I wholeheartedly accepted her position and wished her healing, a long life, and peace.

She left me a voice message the next day apologizing for not being able to make it to see my girls prior to her trip, however she had hoped that it may be different in the future.

I continued crying for several days. I openly shared the message she left, her state of health, and the conversation we had with my three kids.

I asked my girls if they wanted to visit their grandmother prior to her leaving for Iran. I was even willing to take my girls to my husband's sister's home, in the event that this would be the end of life for their grandmother.

My girls did not.
My girls wanted to respect their grandmother's wishes of not wanting to see them.
My girls did not see a reason for calling her to wish her farewell.

At some point, I got done crying.
I had done all that I was able.
I had given it all that I could and then more.

I wish I could have had the capability to get different results.
I wish I could have gifted redemption.
I wish I could have created communion.
I could not have.

I am proud of loving myself to be able to love my husband's mother.
I am proud of being compassionate with myself to be able to be compassionate with my husband's parents.
I am proud of respecting myself to be able to stand strong in front of those who unfoundedly attacked my husband's being.

I am proud of energetically releasing my late husband's family to be able to be released by my late husband's family.

GOD   bless Humanity.
I   bless Humanity.
LOVE bless Humanity.

How to Help

At the beginning:

1. Show up. Show up and take care of whatever is needed.
2. Sit next to. Be there to be held.
3. Give warm calming drinks. Lavender Tea. Saffron Tea. Chamomile Tea.
4. Give warm, soothing meals. Soups. Mashed potatoes.
5. Give space. Give Love. Give Compassion.
6. Take for walks and listen.
7. Share deep sorrow.
8. Talk about the deceased. Share memories.
9. Send a card.
10. Create a fund to help family.
11. Put money in an envelope to give instead of flowers.
12. Create a meal train for the family. Start meals one to two weeks after passing for a period of three months, two times per week.
13. Help with funeral planning and details.
14. Ask guests to write memories of deceased to turn into a memory book for the family.

In the early months:

1. Show up and clean the house.
2. Show up and bring groceries.
3. Show up and take the kids on an outing.
4. Show up and sit with.
5. Show up and brainstorm on what needs to get done.
6. Help make the call for grief counseling.
7. Help accomplish any financial benefit tasks.

In the first year:

1. Show up for support.
2. Check in regularly to instill you've got their back.
3. Make sure grief therapy is continued.
4. Check in to help unclutter home.
5. Check in to assist in going through the deceased's belongings.
6. Show up to help with tombstone details.
7. Show up to handle car maintenance.
8. Check in at milestones. First Birthdays. First Anniversaries. Graduations or First Day of School.
9. Talk about the deceased. Share memories.
10. Show up to take the bereaved out to eateries.
11. Take for walks.
12. Listen.
13. Give support and suggestions for sleepless nights.
14. Share soothing music to heal the deep pain.
15. Encourage writing/creating/art as a form of healing.
16. Encourage self-care as a form of healing.
17. Brainstorm on how the pain can be transformed to help others.
18. Give Love.
19. Give Compassion.
20. Give Understanding.

For more details visit www.SurvivorBenefits.net

About the Cover

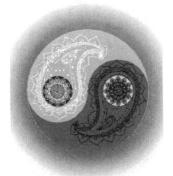

Persian Myth says that the Platycladus Tree (had been filled with pride. The more it grew upward, the more it saw itself higher than others. Once it neared God, up in the skies, the Platycladus Tree realized how insignificant it truly was in relation to all of creation. This awareness made the Platycladus Tree bow its' head all the way back down to earth in *groundedness*. Thus, the Paisley.

The Chinese concept of Yin and Yang is profound for me. There is lightness in darkness and darkness in lightness. In today's polarization of good vs. evil and right vs. wrong, I feel more gravitated towards this concept of interdependency.

This work of art was a labor of love created by Mana Nahavandian, an award-winning Creative Marketing professional.

Made in the USA
San Bernardino, CA
12 September 2018